HIGH SCHOOL WORK STUDY PROGRAM
FOR THE RETARDED

(Second Printing)

HIGH SCHOOL WORK STUDY PROGRAM FOR THE RETARDED

Practical Information for Teacher Preparation and Program Organization and Operation

By

KENNETH H. FREELAND, M.S.

Supervisor, Special Educational Services
Board of Cooperative Educational Services
First Supervisory District, Erie County
Buffalo, New York

Former Teacher-Coordinator
School Work Study Program
Lancaster Central School District
Lancaster, New York

Illustrations by
Roger G. Reuillard

CHARLES C THOMAS · PUBLISHER

Springfield · Illinois · U.S.A.

Published and Distributed Throughout the World by

CHARLES C THOMAS • PUBLISHER

BANNERSTONE HOUSE

301-327 East Lawrence Avenue, Springfield, Illinois, U.S.A.

ISBN 0-398-00611-3

Library of Congress Catalog Card Number: 69-16880

First Printing, 1969
Second Printing, 1974

With THOMAS BOOKS *careful attention is given to all details of manufacturing and design. It is the Publisher's desire to present books that are satisfactory as to their physical qualities and artistic possibilities and appropriate for their particular use.* THOMAS BOOKS *will be true to those laws of quality that assure a good name and good will.*

Printed in the United States of America
00-2

This Book Is Dedicated To
My Dear Grandmother
MARY B. GALLOWAY

PREFACE

This book hopefully will be of interest to the many school and non-school personnel concerned with school work study programming for secondary educable mentally retarded students. It was written because of a recognized need for a work of this type in the field.

This presentation is directed to the teacher in preparation for the challenging task ahead. It is possible that teacher-coordinators on the search for new ideas to improve their respective programs may find this material helpful.

Through its contents the people entrusted with the responsibility for these programs within the school, as well as the people dealing with care and rehabilitation of handicapped youth outside the school, not only may gain a greater insight into the program's organization and operation but also may develop a new perspective into the roles and duties of the teacher involved.

The majority of the reports and forms included in this work have been field-tested, and they are recommended for program use. Teachers, administrators, and supervisors interested in reproducing them for this reason are most welcome to do so upon written permission from both the publisher and the author.

Certainly a book of this size and scope will not provide all the answers. However, if some of the suggestions, devices, and aids contained herein can head the reader in the right direction, then the primary objective for this presentation will have been fulfilled.

ACKNOWLEDGMENTS

My appreciation to Roger Reger, Director of Special Educational Services, Board of Cooperative Educational Services, First Supervisory District, Erie County, Buffalo, New York, whose keen administrative leadership prompted the writing of this book.

For permission to use papers and tables published previously, I wish to thank Carolyn Dobbs, Editor, *The Pointer,* The Association for Special Class Teachers and Parents of the Handicapped; and L. R. Linsenmayer, Chief of State Services and Standards, Bureau of Labor Standards, U. S. Department of Labor.

A note of thanks to Harry Page Decker, Jr., and to Yorktowne Institutional Furniture for permission to reproduce illustrations.

A special "thank you" to my colleagues, Dorothy McCabe and Jean Millholland, for their assistance. Also, to staff artist, Roger Reuillard and to secretaries Mary Malley, June Hoover and Marion Barndollar, for their untiring efforts in manuscript preparation.

I wish also to give acknowledgment to Dr. Allen H. Kuntz and Anthony V. D'Amore for their cooperation in the past regarding school work study, and to the New York State Teacher-Coordinators of Vocational Industrial Cooperative Programs whose publication provided this writer with a beginning format for this presentation.

KENNETH H. FREELAND

CONTENTS

HIGH SCHOOL WORK STUDY PROGRAM
FOR THE RETARDED

KNOW YOUR PROGRAM

Background and Current Interest

School work study programs for the retarded are not new. Brewer[2] indicates that they have been known to special education for approximately the past thirty years.

With the passing of the Vocational Education Act of 1963 and the recent Vocational Education Amendments Act of 1968, interest has reached new heights. Many new programs are priority items on chief school administrators' agendas across the country. We can expect many new innovations in this field, with new exciting programs opening for creative and competent personnel entering this vital phase of education for the educable mentally retarded youth in our secondary schools.

In recent years, the school work study program has taken on various shapes and forms in organizational structure. There are school terminal programs in operation that

1. Operate independently with little or no outside assistance from divisions of vocational rehabilitation and community agencies.
2. Operate in cooperation solely with community employment agencies.
3. Have entered into contractual cooperative agreements with divisions of vocational rehabilitation.
4. Operate with special rehabilitation units in cooperation with divisions of vocational rehabilitation.
5. Have ventured into cooperative programs with sheltered workshops.
6. Have ventured into cooperative programs with sheltered

workshops and the division of vocational rehabilitation.

7. Are operated by special educational services divisions under boards of cooperative educational services which in turn cooperate with divisions of vocational rehabilitation, sheltered workshops, and rehabilitation centers.

Switzer[28] has cited other examples of coordinated programs which have been developed in areas ranging from North Carolina and Alabama to Michigan and South Dakota. Our former Commissioner of the Vocational Rehabilitation Administration and now head of the new Social and Rehabilitation Service has further indicated that programs of this type have spread to almost every state in our nation. With this spreading these programs have assumed various names, and a particular need has arisen for some standard terminology concerning them.

Definition of Terms

Younie[40] has listed six terms often used to refer to terminal programs offering some type of work understanding for the mentally retarded. He feels that these terms, listed below, apparently have been borrowed from general education.

1. Occupational education
2. Pre-vocational training
3. School work experience
4. School work study
5. Work experience
6. Work training

To stimulate the reader toward some clarification in terminology used for these programs, consider work experience and work training as two separate components—perhaps as the two basic phases which would make up the school work study program. Examine Table I, which illustrates the working definitions as providing the basis for this thinking.

To provide you with some background concerning the basic characteristics of the work study program, analyze the program described below which is being used in the New York State area. This program is not the ultimate as far as work study programs are concerned; however, it is an effective one and does provide certain

TABLE I

WORK EXPERIENCE AND WORK TRAINING—THE TWO BASIC COMPONENTS OF THE SCHOOL WORK STUDY PROGRAM

School Work Study Program

Includes the name for the total program. Would include the components below, work experience and work training, with other innovations incorporated.

Work Experience	*Work Training*
Referred to the in-school work phase with remuneration for student efforts. Phase not aimed toward job competency but more concerned with developing general work skills, good work habits, appreciation, and introduction to work. This phase should capitalize on social interaction that takes place between student workers, fellow employees, and employers. Any problems arising here can be filtered back to the classroom for discussion and action where they might be used as realistic learning experiences to be shared by the group. Examples of work would include cafeteria work, bus washing, office jobs, and laundry work (all in-school jobs).	Referred to the out-of-school work phase with at least the minimum wage paid. Students referred to as "trainees" in specific training for a job. Placement is made with reference to student's aptitude and desire and within the realistic occupational goals of students served. Training to be done in the community or in proximity thereof and to be accompanied by a training guideline either provided by the respective employer or located or prepared by the teacher-coordinator. Training is supplemented within the classroom when needed on an individual basis. Examples of training might include training programs in industry, state apprentice programs, and various training projects.[9]

illustrative features[10] which will later be questioned for your better understanding.

Features of the Work Study Program

COMMUNITY. Current population is 30,000. Total school population is 6,100. The major portion of the labor force is trained in manufacturing techniques. The balance is professional, retail, and administration. Wage scales vary from $3.00 per hour for skilled workers to $1.60 for unskilled. Good labor relations in local plants have often been commended. Unions are effective in this area for promoting good working conditions and good production.

CLASS LOCATION. The senior high school in which the class meets is in a centralized school district. The self-contained class accommodates special class students from two nearby school districts. Room size is 50 by 23 feet.

PROCEDURES FOR ADMISSION. Age must be from sixteen to twenty-one years. Most students are accepted from junior high class in special education sequence, but transfers from other districts are accepted. No formal screening procedure is administered. The special education coordinator meets with teachers prior to coming school year to discuss student placement. The teacher-coordinator receives a listing of each new student's pre-vocational skills prior to coming school year. IQ must range from 50 to 75.

PROGRESSION STEPS. Most students have entered the special class at a primary level. There are four levels of progression: primary, intermediate, junior high, and school work study. The terminal phase is five years. For the first two years, students spend one-half day in class and one-half day on job in-school work experience with pay. The next two years can include one-half day in class and one-half day work training within the community with pay, or one-half day in school and one-half day in an exploratory vocational program at a nearby vocational center, or a combination of both. The last year, students are placed full-time in work training in the community until graduation. The program is flexible, and students may leave the program early, depending upon their success and readiness to enter the work world.

CURRICULUM. The curriculum is oriented toward social, personal, academic, and occupational development. Academics are practical and applied to everyday living and needs. Correlation of work experience and work training with academic instruction is accomplished as much as possible. Teachers use an overview guide which they have prepared. The class moves as group to special subject areas for home economics, physical education, wood shop, and art.

EQUIPMENT. Office space attached to the classroom contains files, desk, typewriter, telephone, resource materials, and personal professional library. The classroom has a supplemental home economics area, a shop area, and a science table, including all the necessary equipment. There is a good grooming area with full length mirror. A library corner provides for small reading groups. Ample storage space is allotted for teacher-made materials and texts. The teacher is allowed $500 per year to purchase supplies.

GENERAL DESCRIPTION. The classroom can accommodate twenty-five students comfortably. Scheduling is arranged by teacher and principal. Class hours are from 8 A.M. to 2:30 P.M. Class remains in session in the mornings until 11 A.M. Most students return during the last period of the day for instruction after half-day work experience or training is completed. The teacher is free daily for almost two hours to coordinate the program.

INTEGRATION. Extracurricular activities are open to students. Class attends morning assemblies when scheduled. Individual students attend regular classes if they are capable and can benefit from instruction. Students take physical education and eat lunch with regular students.

TRANSPORTATION. Arrangements for out-of-district students are made by the Special Services Coordinator. Each district is responsible for its own transportation arrangements. Students are transported to vocational centers and work experience sites through provisions made by their home schools. Students in the full-time work training phase usually arrange their own transportation.

WORK EXPERIENCE PHASE. Two of the three participating districts provide job sites for pupils. Jobs include cafeteria work (all types), building maintenance, grounds maintenance, bus washing, bus sweeping, laundry work, and office work. Students are paid the federal mandatory wage for school employees unless exempted. Participating districts budget $8,000 for this phase of the program. The teacher prepares and submits the payroll list to the business office. Pay checks are distributed to the class every two weeks. Student incomes are correlated realistically within the budgeting and wise-spending phase of the curriculum.

WORK TRAINING PHASE. Community business and industry are receptive to the program. Area golf-course superintendents are involved in the project to train workers.[7] Local contractors have trained students in a State Apprentice Program. The teacher-coordinator maintains a file of training materials to supplement training on an individual basis in classroom. Students receive at least the minimum wage during the training phase. They may enter a multivocational exploratory program for one year; this includes food-service preparation, gas station operation, building maintenance, grounds maintenance, nurses aide work, mail room operations, and assembly and benchwork. If recommended, students may enter the two-year vocational program.

COUNSELING. Counseling is done by the teacher-coordinator, supervisor, school guidance counselor, and vocational counselor at the center.

PLACEMENT PROVISIONS. The teacher-coordinator is responsible for job placements. Teacher-coordinators of vocational industrial cooperative programs exchange job leads. Difficult students to place are referred to the State Division of Vocational Rehabilitation (DVR) for vocational evaluations and other services. The teacher-coordinator and supervisor assist the DVR counselor in securing on-the-job training sites for students referred. The supervisor maintains close contact with rehabilitation centers where students are undergoing various phases of training. The program has averaged approximately 80 per cent of its own placements annually.

CERTIFICATES. Students are recommended by the teacher-coordinator for completion of program certificates to the Special Educational Services Division. No written criteria or standards are in effect. Certificates are presented at home school graduation or district-wide ceremony for all special class pupils completing the program.

FOLLOW-UP. This is the responsibility of the supervisor, who also works as advisor to all programs under the jurisdiction of the Special Educational Services Division.

SUPERVISION. The teacher-coordinator is responsible for supervision of his students on various jobs. Teacher-coordinators are observed and evaluated by the Special Education Curriculum Coordinator, who also gives advice on current curriculum materials available and gives guidance in ordering supplies.

IN-SERVICE WORK AND MEETINGS. The teacher-coordinator attends local educational institutes as organized during the year by the Special Education Director and the Curriculum Coordinator. The teacher-coordinator attends curriculum and in-service meetings. He also attends a monthly meeting with other teacher-coordinators of nearby school districts under the Special Educational Services Division as arranged by the supervisor. The teacher-coordinator attends local high school meetings as directed by the building principal.

PARENT PARTICIPATION. Parents meet with a larger parent group composed of three school districts. Parents supply occasional training leads to the program. Parents attend individual conferences when scheduled and are urged to contact the teacher-coordinator regarding particular work problems. Special class report cards are sent home at regular high school reporting intervals.

The particular program just described was originally initiated by the home school district involved. In recent years, this district—like many progressive districts in the country—has entered into a cooperative agreement with the local Board of Cooperative Educational Services.[10] This program is one of the many varied responsibilities of the director of the Special Educational Services Division under this cooperating board.

To generate comments regarding programs which you have been familiar with and ones which you will be seeing in the future, and to broaden your background, consider the following questions regarding the program outlined:

1. What seem to be the outstanding features of this program?
2. Can you locate certain weaknesses within the framework?
3. Why do you think this program might be effective?
4. How would you compare it to programs you have seen?
5. What questions would you like to ask the teacher-coordinator in charge?
6. What features would you consider changing?
7. What features give you clues to the underlying work study philosophy in operation?
8. Does the job placement per cent figure on students leaving the program reflect the true success of the program?
9. Do you think a program of this type would operate in your particular community?

In your conscientious attempt to answer the above questions, it is hoped that you have gained somewhat of a new perspective into the features encompassed in the school work study operation. To know your program, you should be able to analyze these areas, to capitalize further on its strong points, and to pinpoint and remedy its weak areas.

Moreover, you may be housed in a high school or district that has work study programs for regular class students. It would be wise to become acquainted with the features involved in these programs and to note how they fit into the total school program. They may be disguised under various titles, but briefly they include[37] the following:

1. *The Vocational Commercial Cooperative Program:* This provides combined instruction in the classroom and training on-the-job to develop vocational competence for office skills.
2. *The Vocational Distributive Cooperative Program:* This provides for classroom instruction and work training

through employment in behind-the-counter and other mer-
chandising jobs.

3. *The Vocational Industrial Cooperative Program:* This provides a combination of related general information and related trade theory, together with supervised training in
approved places of employment. The program provides instruction and training involving manipulative skills in trade
and technical vocations.

Get to know the teacher-coordinators of these programs. Many
of these gentlemen possess much know-how and have much to
offer regarding training and community information. Work on a
cooperative basis with them regarding various job leads, and do
not encroach upon their training areas. Make a note to review the
features and objectives of their programs.

Some of our more mature and more adept special class pupils
have moved out of the terminal retarded program and through
these programs with reasonable success. The more familiar you
can become with the various programs operating around you, the
better equipped you will be to form a comprehensive picture of
your own program and its needs.

Discussion Problems and Activities

1. Trace the history of special education in your state and
note how school work study programs evolved for the educable mentally retarded.
2. Secure and compare copies of various cooperative plans of
operation between school systems and the state divisions of
vocational rehabilitation.
3. What is a Special Rehabilitation Unit?
4. Regarding effectiveness, what must you know about school
work study programs that operate independently—with no
outside assistance?
5. Special Educational Service is one of the major services
offered to cooperating school districts by boards of cooperative educational services. What other major services are
also offered? Could these services have a bearing on your
work study program?

6. List the services for the retarded provided by your State Division of Vocational Rehabilitation.
7. Discuss what constitutes an effective pre-vocational program. How does this area fit in with the work study program?
8. Locate copies of various special education philosophies regarding school work study programs and compare them. Where do they differ? If so, how can you explain this?
9. What constitutes the vocational rehabilitation philosophy?
10. The new Social and Rehabilitation Services represents a major reorganization in the Department of Health, Education, and Welfare. It has five major agencies. List them and their respective responsibilities.

Chapter II

KNOW THE OBJECTIVES AND VALUES OF YOUR PROGRAM—AND YOUR RESPONSIBILITIES

Successful work study programs seem to have one common element. At the helm of the program, they have a competent teacher-coordinator who is dedicated to his job: he knows his program's objectives and values, and he has an adequate understanding of his basic responsibilities. Let us begin this section by touching lightly on the subject of objectives for the program.

General and Specific Objectives

The general objectives for special education are the same for all students. They would include the following as listed by the Educational Policies Commission: [19]

1. The Objectives of Self-Realization
2. The Objectives of Human Relationships
3. The Objectives of Economic Efficiency
4. The Objectives of Civic Responsibilities

Each of the cardinal objectives listed above is broken down more precisely into subgroups that will provide the teacher-coordinator with additional background in this area. Also worth attention is the listing by the Educational Policies Commission[18] of objectives for all American youth. Each secondary special class teacher's plan book should include a copy of this report.

In discussing specific objectives for your program, you must keep in focus your particular students' needs and the nature of the community where the program is housed. Objectives must be formulated by the instructor and must guide his planning throughout the school year. It is good practice to list the particular objec-

12

tives you are trying to achieve daily. In the school work study program, most of your subject area objectives will be directed toward the world of work. You will notice that the examples given below of specific objectives in this direction are behaviorally oriented for the students and are not objectives for the teachers.*

Closely related to your objectives, you might consider the values of your program. What might these include for the student, the school, and the community? You may be out in the community some evening at the speaker's stand fielding questions regarding this phase of the program. Be prepared.

Values to Students

1. Students have an opportunity to explore various jobs for work experience and training.
2. Students develop appreciation and respect for work.
3. As wage earners, students have the opportunity to handle and budget their own money realistically.
4. Students have the opportunity to learn useful work skills on real jobs under actual working conditions and to bring their problems back to the classroom for discussion and guidance.[38]
5. The student's transition from school to the work world is a guided and smooth one.

---

*This approach seems to have merit not only for specific planning but for accomplishing the objective.

Subject Area	Specific Objective
Citizenship	To have students see the importance, as workers, of taking care of company property and tools.
Health	To have students develop an awareness that care of teeth is important to them as workers.
Arithmetic	To have students identify the differences between "gross" and "net" pay.
Reading	To have students identify the days of the week and their abbreviations from a group of words on a wall chart.
Spelling	To have students realize that correct spelling on application forms is essential.
Penmanship	To have students see a demonstration on why certain workers need to write legibly.
Shop	To have students develop the awareness that there is a correct tool for each job.
Home economics	To have students see why the correct storage of food is important to the health of the worker.
Safety	To have students (via pictures) see the various jobs that require safety glasses to be worn.
Social studies	To have students hear (via tape recorder) about the various social insurances available to the worker.

6. Students are acquainted with, and learn, the necessary work qualities of a successful worker.[38]
7. Students acquire the attitudes, habits, and skills essential for employability.

Values to the School

1. The school can more realistically approach educational objectives.
2. Equipment and facilities beyond financial reach of the school are utilized.[37]
3. The school is able to provide work training with minimum expense.
4. Skills and knowledge of individuals outside the school are coordinated in the training of students.[37]
5. The program helps bring the community and the school closer together.
6. The program helps to meet the dropout problem and increases the holding power of the school.

Values to the Community

1. The community gets eventual taxpayers.
2. The community gets contributing citizens.
3. Employers have the opportunity to train their own workers with cooperation of the school.
4. Business and industry have the opportunity to participate in a community service.[37]

Although research on existing programs is limited, current practice does seem to suggest that the school work study concept is the most effective approach to programming for our educable retarded at the secondary school level.[10]

Beekman,[1] one of the pioneers and leaders in the field, has stated the social values offered by programs where retarded youth can open an avenue of communication with the elite majority, the people who work for a living. In doing so, the program for the retarded becomes a measure of self-respect and personal worth, apart from its intrinsic value as a means for his livelihood.

Karnes[11] feels that the fullest values of such programs have not been determined. Many in the field are awaiting needed studies to give more information on the vocational and social adjustments of the retarded who have and have not been provided with special educational programs.

We do, however, have information that one of the keys to an effective program is the teacher. Unfortunately, few teachers arrive on the site of the program fully prepared for the position of teacher-coordinator. As you will see, the required competencies are varied and many. Perhaps, as a start, a clarification of the term *teacher-coordinator* would be helpful.

Required Competencies and Responsibilities
of the Teacher-Coordinator

The term "teacher-coordinator" is used because the man charged with the responsibility of the program must be much more than a special education teacher. The French gentleman who originated the phrase *homme 'a tout faire* (jack-of-all-trades) surely had this task in mind at inception. The teacher-coordinator is concerned with all aspects of the program in school and with the important liaison activities affiliated with it. He spends part of the day teaching and correlating instruction in the classroom, and part of the day coordinating his program in and outside of school in a variety of roles.

The foregoing description seems to indicate a special person for this job. Examine with me the following combination of factors: professional preparation, desired experience, desired competencies, and the respective responsibilities this important position dictates.

The literature has not indicated any special certificates or requirements for the job at this time. Most certification requirements seem to include graduation from an accredited college or university with a degree in elementary or secondary education, with completion of courses related to exceptional children and the required courses in the field of education for the mentally retarded.[33] Desirable college courses in public speaking, occupational information, and counseling would also be helpful.

Prior successful teaching experience with a mentally retarded group at a lower level, and a good understanding of the total program, would be most helpful. Some industrial work experience or a good background knowledge of the world of work and its problems would also be beneficial. In addition to this experience, there are certain qualities and skills the teacher-coordinator should possess. Campbell, Corbally, and Ramseyer[3] have indicated that there is increasing evidence that a person with certain abilities for a specific assignment has a better chance of success if he is qualified. It seems logical to assume that a person is more comfortable and will possibly gain more happiness and eventual success from a position for which he is best suited than he will by attempting to succeed where he lacks certain prerequisites.

Rather than elaborate on this aspect at length but still to provide you with some understanding of the qualifications desired, rate yourself on the evaluation sheet provided as Table II. Please use the rating scale included and omit the last section since this area can only fairly be administered while you are participating in the field. Hopefully, this exercise will provide you with some additional preparation material and a chance to get to know yourself a little better. It is assumed that you possess all necessary characterologic and mental attributes expected of all our teachers. A score of 115 or more might suggest that you have real potential for the challenging responsibility ahead.

The duties of the teacher-coordinator are numerous and diversified. He must be a versatile and talented individual. He must have the ability to adapt to a variety of roles and situations.[37] The need for adaptability can be indicated by the following list of responsibilities often designated to this person in the performance of his work[33]:

1. Provides systematic classroom instruction.
2. Plans an instructional program.
3. Reviews case histories and results of appropriate tests.
4. Selects and devises instructional techniques, materials, and equipment.
5. Surveys business, schools, and industry for job sites.
6. Provides suitable job placement for students.
7. Interviews prospective employers.
8. Prepares students for job interviews and for the world of work.
9. Locates, prepares, and utilizes training materials.

TABLE II

TEACHER-COORDINATOR EVALUATION SHEET

_____
Name

_____
Date

Social, Personal, Mental, and Physical Qualities

Appearance		Understanding	
Health		Maturity	
Initiative		Open-mindedness	
Integrity		Courteousness	
Dependability		Cooperativeness	
Enthusiasm		Flexibility	
Adaptability		Patience	
Creativity		Friendliness	
Sociability		Persistence	

Professional Skills, Qualities, and Techniques

Understanding of youth and needs		Understanding of responsibilities	X
Understanding of EMR objectives		Professional interest	X
Lesson-planning		Organization	X
Understanding of methods		Judgment	X
Understanding of materials		Ability to correlate instruction	X
Understanding of curriculum		Individual instruction	X
Interest in students		Prompt reports	X
Scholarship		Accurate reports	X
Objectivity		Supervision of workers	X
Special ed. philosophy		Job placement	X
Work study philosophy		Public relations	X
Discipline		Counseling	X

Scale .... Superior 5
Above average 4
Average 3
Below average 2
Fair 1

Total_____

10. Supervises students on job sites.
11. Distributes, collects, evaluates, and utilizes work progress reports.
12. Correlates work experience and training in the classroom.
13. Makes referrals to community agencies when required.
14. Keeps accurate work study records.
15. Provides individual and group counseling.
16. Provides for parent conferences and meetings.
17. Provides a "school-public information" plan for the program.
18. Prepares periodic reports, evaluations, and recommendations.
19. Maintains close lines of communication with personnel concerned with the program.
20. Prepares and submits work study payroll for students when required.
21. Maintains effective public relations.

Discussion Problems and Activities

1. What objectives do you feel would be most difficult to achieve in the work study classroom?
2. List the objectives you feel would require the need for greater innovation on the part of the teacher-coordinator.
3. Some values of the work study program for students have been indicated. Can you list any disadvantages the program may present to the students involved?
4. Prepare a guideline of the characteristics of the educable mentally retarded at the secondary level.
5. Make a list of the members who compose the rehabilitation team. What are their basic functions and responsibilities?
6. Discuss this statement, "The teacher-coordinator of the work study program for retarded youth should have specific certification requirements."
7. What people make up the interdisciplinary team?
8. Locate, examine, and discuss the qualifications for the rehabilitation counselor and the social worker.
9. What specific positions in the armed forces might help in the preparation of a teacher-coordinator?

10. Can you give an example of *imbalance* of any of the social or personal qualities that might be to your disadvantage in applying for the position of teacher-coordinator?
11. What particular qualities might you add to the evaluation sheet for the teacher-coordinator?
12. List the advantages for the teacher-coordinator who lives in the community where his program is housed.
13. What professional organizations might assist the teacher-coordinator in his professional growth?
14. Compile a listing of the periodicals which the new teacher-coordinator might include on his reading list.
15. What are the specific requirements in your state for teaching the educable mentally retarded? Are they the same for teaching secondary retarded students?

Chapter III

ORGANIZING YOUR PROGRAM

As a beginning teacher-coordinator, be prepared to organize a new program. If the need arises, you must plan each step accordingly. There are certain principles involved, but move deliberately at this period and know where you are headed and why. Remember, this is the foundation of your program. It only will be as strong as you make it in this vital stage. Some suggestions which may prove helpful are discussed below.

Setting Up a New Program

First, if you were hired for this job, it is apparent that the school administration has realized the important need for this program. This is a major step in the right direction. Secondly, you may find that the school administrators have specific views on the particular type of program they want initiated. You may have to regulate your plan to incorporate their views. Some of our school leaders are well-advised in this phase. They may have made visitations to various districts to see programs in operation and, in turn, have evaluated them and have certain ideas concerning their respective organization. Keep these ideas in mind; if possible, get them in writing since they will be helpful in setting up your respective guidelines. On the other hand, the school administration may suggest that you present the plan (with assistance or not) to them for approval. Whatever the approach used, here are some points for your consideration.

First and foremost are the students to be served. Get to know them and their particular needs. If you have the opportunity to work with them in a classroom before setting up the program, this is in your favor. If you will not have this opportunity, meet with the previous junior high teacher and together scrutinize the individual student cumulative record folders. Make individual notes as you seek out the information on the students to be served. Secure some pre-vocational rating forms and have the former teacher rate each student in this area. Any other information with reference to work habits, work skills, or particular aptitudes will be extremely helpful to you. You will also be concerned with up-to-date data on mental ages, IQ's, test dates, type of tests used, achievement scores in reading, spelling, arithmetic, and language. Chronological ages when students entered special program, student medications, physical defects, and evaluations concerning their social and emotional maturities and manual dexterities should be included. Also, find out if each student has worked around the neighborhood and/or around the home. Individual interviews at home with the students and parents will give you additional information into their particular occupational goals, whether they be realistic or otherwise. The home visits can be very helpful, and data obtained will aid you not only in the instructional phase of your program but also will provide some helpful background for your initial work placements. I repeat, if you have the opportunity to work with these youngsters the year this program is in the planning stage, you will be off on firmer ground with a keener understanding of their particular needs.

Next, make a *general* survey of the community—general, in a sense, because you are not concerned specifically at this time with immediate out-of-school job placement leads. These leads will come later. If you are new in the community, contact the town or city hall and procure a brochure and gather some basic facts regarding population, labor organizations, chambers of commerce, service groups, rehabilitation centers, community agencies, employment services, and the industrial life of the community.

In the near future, it will be advisable to gain more knowledge on local conditions in the community with regard to local work training opportunities, trends in business, industrial development, and recent openings in new employment. When this time comes, meet with the local teacher-coordinator of the work study program for the regular high school students. If there is none available in your high school, check the district nearby. Develop lines of communication with this person and set up an exchange of job leads with him. Many times, he secures various job openings that may fall within the ranges and abilities of your group and vice versa. If he invites you to attend one of their group meetings, do not refuse. These men are quite up-to-date on community trends, labor and union regulations, and have much to offer the newcomer. Do not alienate them by moving into their training sites in the community without their prior knowledge or approval. Impersonal interviews with some of the "town fathers" can also broaden your perspective of this important survey.

At this point, you are ready to start canvassing the various schools in your district to see what work experience sites are available. Before this is accomplished, or even during, go out of your way to meet the various supervisors in charge of cafeterias, transportation, building, ground maintenance, and laundry departments. On your tour of the system, make notes concerning names of business managers, payroll managers, and building principals; jot down the names of the various cafeteria managers and head custodians in each building. During the introductions, make some mental notes and see what jobs may be available. Be alert, for you might have to create some jobs that are not in existence.

In your travels about the schools, become familiar with the individuals who make up the pupil personnel service areas such as the psychological, guidance, health, and attendance services. When you are ready to incorporate a screening policy into your program, you will need the assistance of these people, plus your fellow teachers and building principal to develop standards for admission and possible alternatives to students who may fail to qualify for the program. Some students may not be ready socially, emotionally, physically, or occupationally for secondary placement at this particular time.

Meet with your building principal regarding special subject areas for your students, as well as ways of integrating your students within the total high school program. Specifically indicate the assistance needed by all the aforementioned individuals and describe in your plan how these persons can help. A minor illustration of this would be the school nurse's role at the high school level. She could include the scheduling of your group's physical exams for working papers during the summer months when the varsity football squad reports for annual examination. This necessary task will be out of the way when you start processing employment certificates in the fall.

Now that you have some understanding regarding the students, community, and the school district, you are ready to start organizing your program. If you are still not sure what features to incorporate, make a few visitations to other programs. Scan the literature for effective programs in operation. Ask questions. Write letters. But know beforehand the features you want in your program and be prepared to justify why. If you have certain innovations you want to include, this is commendable; however, keep in mind that programs will differ to meet the unique character and resources of each community.

Your organizational plan should state your objectives; for better planning, break them down specifically for each subject area you are going to include. List your students' needs and be ready to explain how the program will fit within the total development of all the special classes in the district. Review carefully the existing curriculum for all levels. Point up particular areas where you will need the utmost of efforts from your fellow teachers. In turn, they may have some valuable contributions. If you have some critical evaluations to make of the current curriculum, save them. Later, you will have the opportunity to incorporate your suggestions. The progressive special education teachers hold frequent curriculum meetings, and they know that their curriculums must be flexible and are ever-changing. You will have your opportunity. Be patient.

At this point, you are ready to start thinking about finances. In compiling a proposed budget for the necessities of your program, consider the following:

1. Wages for the in-school work experience phase of the program will depend upon the numbers of students involved, total work days per school year, hours per day, and legal wages. Some programs pay student workers out of the cafeteria fund. The question then arises, Who pays bus

washers, laundry workers, office helpers? To alleviate this problem, get the total figure for the entire operation earmarked for this purpose.

2. In addition to the materials needed for the instructional phase of your operation, budget for business supplies (letterhead paper, envelopes, business cards, file folders, forms, stamps, paper clips, etc.) and include an outside telephone on this list. Effective programs cannot afford to operate without this valuable communicative device.

3. Various initial equipment you might want to include in your program will be discussed briefly in the next section. This, however, will depend considerably upon the size of the room that has been set aside for the work study program.

4. In your supervisory role of the program, you will be doing much traveling in your own automobile. For this reason, you should budget for mileage. Each school district has its own policy, along with the necessary forms to claim this reimbursement. A note of caution: check with your insurance agent about driving during business hours. Your rates may increase, so budget for this item. Check also the policy of your school district regarding transporting students for job interviews in your automobile. This factor may also increase your rates.

In your plan, be sure to include the time you will need to supervise and coordinate your program in the afternoon. To justify this aspect, you might include a list of responsibilities which you must perform in connection with your program.

You should also indicate the transportation needed to get your students to and from their in-school jobs. Once you have final approval of your organizational plan, these details can be finalized with the supervisor in charge of transportation. In the meantime, consider what you will need and list the placement sites. In the future when you start your work training placement into the community itself, you might consider the use of public transportation for your young adults. Transportation is a vital cog in the machinery of your program, and any problem will be alleviated considerably if you have the full cooperation of the school administration.

Equally important, include in your plan the community agencies that will provide additional services to your program. Find out what your local division of vocational rehabilitation counselor can do, what the director at the local rehabilitation center can do, and what your local employment service can do to render assistance to your program. You might want to incorporate these features into your program, so it is wise to know what is available and to what degree.

Maybe it would be wise to outline a public information plan for your program. List here how you plan to gain support of parents, teachers, regular students, nonprofessional staff members who will be working side by side with your students, and the community in general. This can be done in a variety of ways, as you will see in the next chapter.

In quick review then, check these items for your organizational plan:

1. Need for program
2. Students' needs
3. Work study objectives
4. Community survey
5. School survey
6. Existing curriculum
7. Screening procedures for program
8. Services and facilities needed
9. Budget items
10. Supervisory time
11. Transportation needs
12. Community agencies available
13. Public information plan
14. Cooperation needed

You may have other points to include. In any event, put them in writing. Have duplicate copies for administrators and board members. Pinpoint each area at the meeting and stress how vital each component is to the total success of the program. Incorporate any valuable ideas suggested by board members and administrators, and make it known that total cooperation is mandatory to get the program off the ground.

Classroom Plan and Equipment

It may not come your first year, or your second, but be ready for the day when the superintendent of your district calls you into his office and asks if you have any ideas about designing your own classroom. This may startle you at first, but once the values of your program are evidenced in the school and the community, be prepared. Many high schools are expanding facilities to meet their increased enrollments, and this trend is not likely to change for some time. In turn, the progressive chief school administrator will be quick to recognize your need for a special facility and will be willing to accommodate this innovation in his building expansion plan if he can.

Of course, the design of the classroom and equipment needed will depend upon the square footage which will be available to you. If the classroom additions are to be all standard size, you will naturally have to plan accordingly. Utilize this space wisely in your planning. It might be helpful to make a list of the specific areas you want to include in the room. Then rank them by priority according to how they fit into your program's objectives and how much they will be used. Discuss this project with the contractor; he may have some suggestions. I suggest that you make a variety of sketches and have them drawn to scale by the contractor's architect. Study them carefully, discuss the variations with your superintendent, and come up with a practical joint decision.

Some of the areas you might include in your plan will be supplemental facilities to what are available in school. In this regard, certain questions must be answered. For instance, your girls may leave as a group for home economics while the boys are in shop. This seems to be routine in scheduling. However, what instruction in home economics do the boys receive? Do you think it is important that your boys have some basics in cooking? You must answer this question. By the same token, consider developing some basic hand skills in a type of handicraft or a small wood-projects program for the girls. Can you visualize a grouping activity where four girls and three boys are involved in a cooking project at one part of the room, while three girls and four boys are in another part of the room busily engaged in wood projects? The boys are proudly relating to the girls what they have learned from their shop teacher, and the girls are sharing their knowledge and displaying their techniques as acquired in their home economics class. The reinforcement of learning that has taken place beforehand exceeds description.

When planning for certain areas where you will be teaching, insure that you will have bulletin boards of sufficient size and chalkboards in these specific locations. They will be invaluable to you. You might also concentrate on your major seating area first. This is where you will be conducting most of your lessons, so plan your other areas around this focal point. Keep in mind that the students can move or turn their desks for lessons at either end of the room.

Be innovative in your design to take full advantage of space and equipment. When you examine Figure 1, note the particular location of the science table in relation to the home economics area. This science table was specially constructed so that the counter area would extend through the cooking area. Here it can be used as a serving location when the class is conducting a social activity in connection with their cooking experience.

In addition, consider the *good grooming* area located in the left-rear corner. However limited, this does provide some privacy for the individual when he or she is getting ready for work. Along these lines, you might have your boys build a medium-sized movable partition to provide the girls with more privacy at the dressing table.

As you can imagine, the small reading group area and the library area can be utilized for many activities. This is a handy corner to have available for all types of grouping instruction. It can also be utilized for small group counseling sessions. If you are interested, include an electrical outlet nearby since excellent use of the tape recorder can be made in this area.

The following is a list of equipment found in the respective areas of Figure 1:

1. General Seating Area	Students desks and chairs, large chalkboard, large tackboard, and teacher's table.
2. Entrance Area	Industrial-type time clock, rack, cards, tackboard for notices, and teacher's closet.
3. Supplemental Home Economics Area	Refrigerator, electric range, sink, cupboard space, work counters.
4. Science Area	Sink, gas, electric outlets, counter top for experiments, storage space for science equipment.
5. Good-grooming Area	Full-length mirror, tackboard, dressing table, shoe-shine kit, etc.
6. Storage Area	Individual compartments with sliding doors for systematic storage of texts, materials, aids, etc.
7. Supplemental Shop Area	Workbench, tool locker, paint booth with exhaust fan, storage cabinet, power jigsaw, and tackboard.
8. Small Group Reading and Library Area	Round table, chairs, bookshelves, chalkboard.
9. Teacher-coordinator's Office	Teacher's desk, chair, file cabinet, extra chair, partition window, typewriter, bookshelves, tackboard, outside telephone, audiovisual equipment storage area, Dutch doors.*

Figures 2 through 7 illustrate the above areas in more detail.

Classroom Organization for Program Instruction

As you become more involved with the instructional phase of the program, you will soon come to recognize one major disadvantage the school work study program presents. The work experience and work training phases where your students are out of the classroom for half a day cut markedly into in-school instructional time. For this reason, it becomes of paramount importance that each minute of classroom instruction be closely accounted for and well spent. The wise instructor will make this time factor known to his students the day school opens. As he briefs his new arrivals and reminds the students returning to the program, he will review their responsibilities and obligations concerning the in-school instructional phase. Time is a vital factor, and hopefully the class will come to realize this and become accustomed to the set organized routines if emphasized repeatedly. In turn, the students will also become accustomed to the demands this approach dictates and will soon find a sense of security in knowing their responsibilities. In addition, they will develop certain desirable work habits that are mandatory for the adult work world.

*Dutch doors were installed so space could be used as a banking facility to help implement this area of the curriculum.

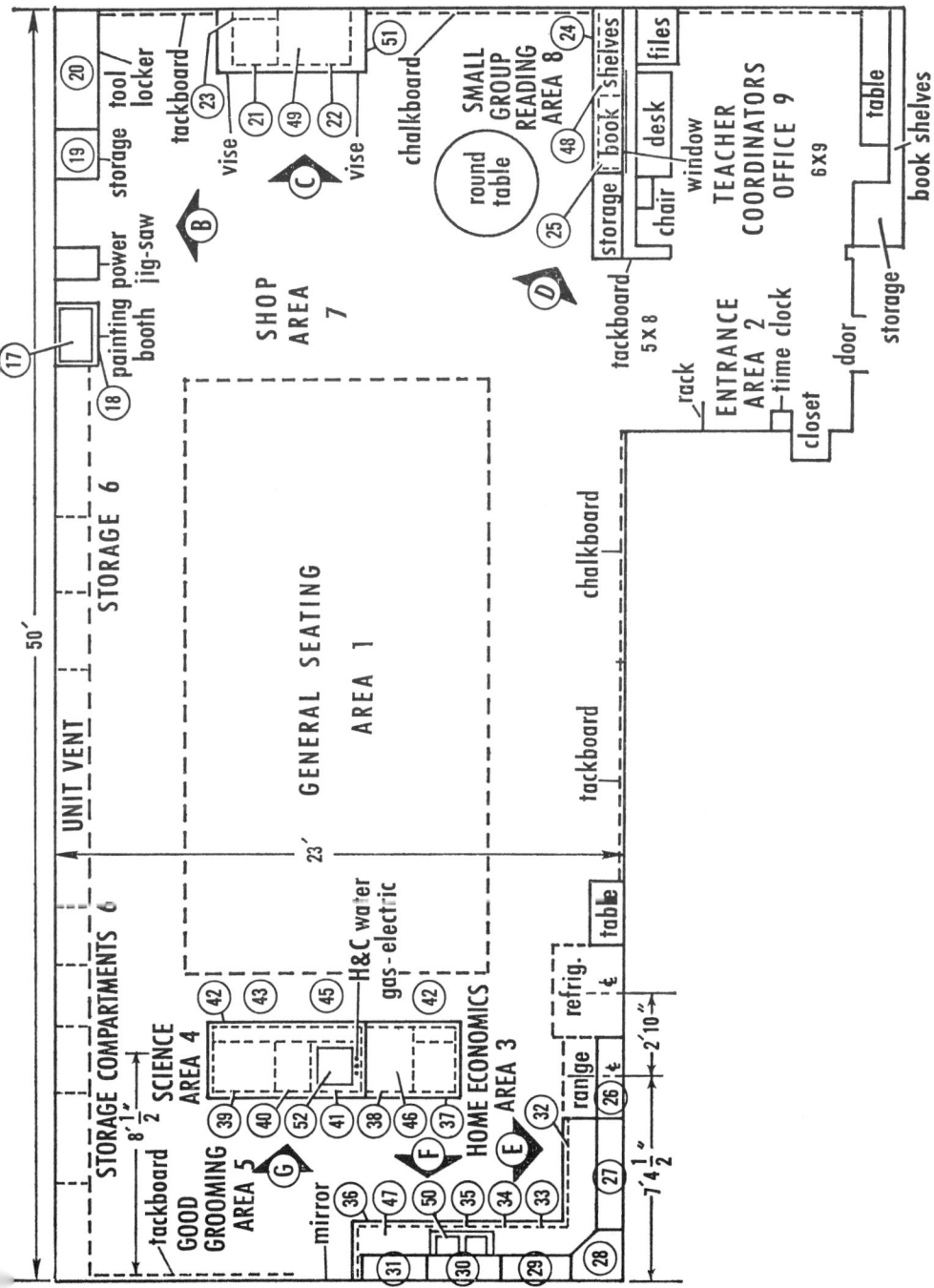

FIGURE 1. School work study classroom designed by author. *Courtesy of York-towne Institutional Furniture.*

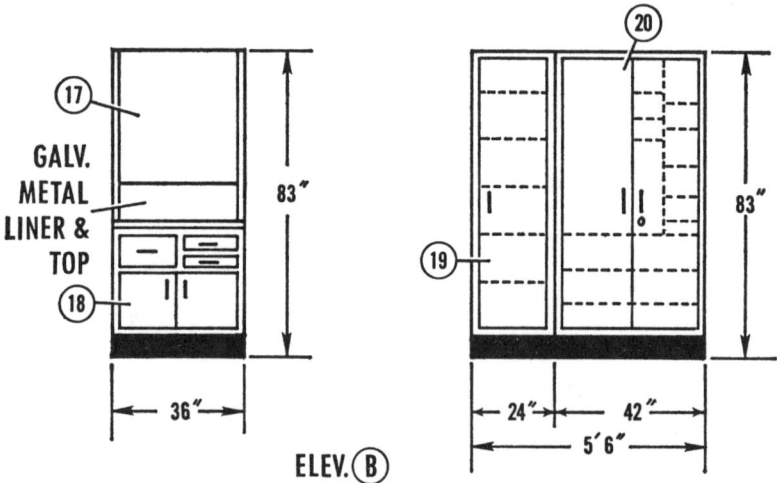

FIGURE 2. Paint locker and tool locker for supplemental shop area. *Courtesy of Yorktowne Institutional Furniture.*

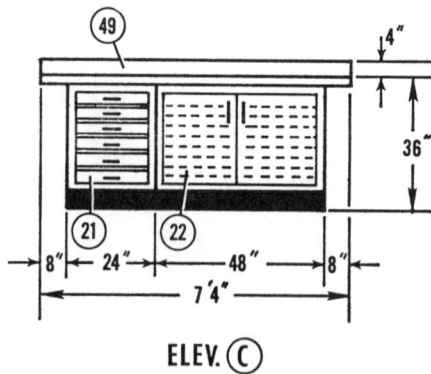

FIGURE 3. Work bench for supplemental shop area. *Courtesy of Yorktowne Institutional Furniture.*

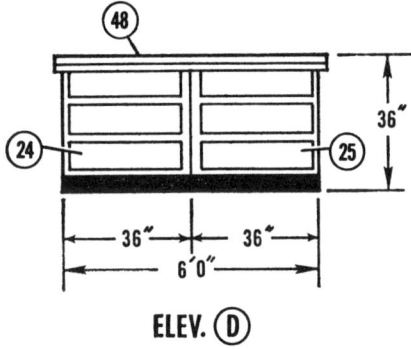

ELEV. Ⓓ

FIGURE 4. Bookshelves for small reading group area. *Courtesy of Yorktowne Institutional Furniture.*

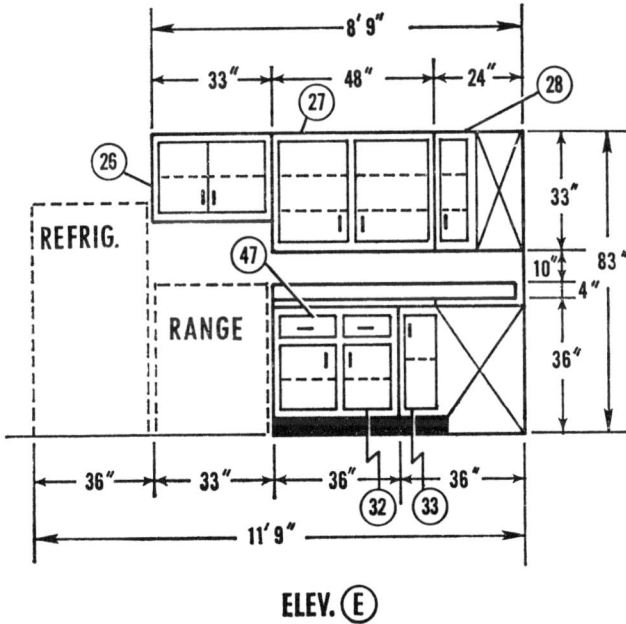

ELEV. Ⓔ

FIGURE 5. Cupboards and work counters for supplemental home economics area. Space indicated for refrigerator and electric range. *Courtesy of Yorktowne Institutional Furniture.*

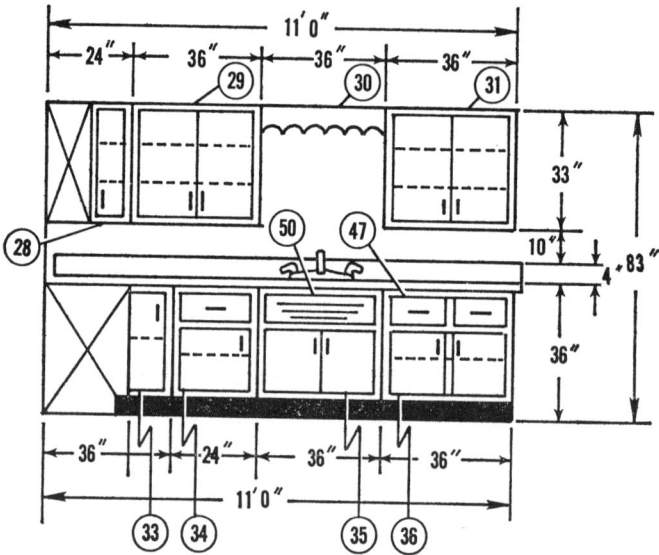

ELEV. (F)

FIGURE 6. Cupboards, work counters, and sink for supplemental home economics area. *Courtesy of Yorktowne Institutional Furniture.*

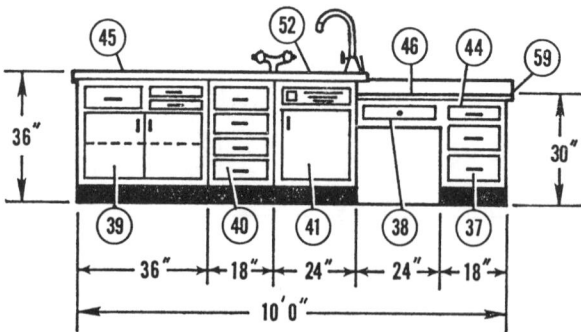

ELEV. (G)

FIGURE 7. *Science area* with additional work and storage space. *Courtesy of Yorktowne Institutional Furniture.*

If you are highly organized in your routines and lessons, you will experience few discipline problems in the classroom since these usually originate when students find time on their hands in a hit-and-miss type of operation. You must develop the technique of moving quickly from one subject area to the next, and this necessitates that your materials are close at hand, you are well-planned, and your students are ready for action. In a sense, you are putting certain pressures on them, but in reality are you not conditioning them for the time element they will face later on their respective jobs?

I am not advocating that you race through your lessons, but I am suggesting that your lessons have a certain tempo that gets you and your group underway and does not stop until your class is excused for work. You are well on your way to good organization when you can look at the clock and say, "We have covered much ground in the three hours allotted this morning." If you have a *bad day** (i.e. are holding up the tempo) and you can sense a reaction from your group which calls out *let's get going,* then you will know that the ultimate in proper pacing and motivation has been reached.

Chances are that you will develop rapport quickly with your group if you are maintaining a satisfactory tempo—and if you are using a combination of firmness, fairness, and consistency. Keep in mind also that they will learn much from your behavior and will likely reflect some of this behavior in their daily living. Consider your courtesy, your work habits, your appearance, your punctuality, your attendance, and the respect you display in dealing with people in and out of the classroom. These are the subtle learnings that take place with continuous repetition. Try making them work positively for you. They cannot help but rub off on your group.

Each school day starts with certain opening exercises and basic routines. Organize them to your advantage. The following are some suggestions:

1. Pledge to the Flag	Bill steps to the front of the class. From the chart on the bulletin board, he knows he leads the group for two weeks.
2. Morning Announcements	Over the intercom system, a student reads the morning announcements. Everyone listens attentively.

*All teachers have them, perhaps due to lack of preparation or materials.

| 3. Teacher-coordinator | Reviews any questions regarding office announcements. Class announcements by teacher or individual students. |
| 4. Morning Weather Report | Alice steps to front of room and gives report via weather-chart board provided. She is the weatherman for the month and gets her information by listening to the radio before coming to school. Information includes the day, the date, the temperature, and the forecast. |

During the weather report, Peter (who is assigned attendance man) checks the time-card rack and informs the teacher of the students absent. Peter receives absentees' attendance cards for delivery to the attendance office. The bell rings, and the first period begins in four minutes.

Since the opening exercises are routine, the daily program must also take on this organized pattern. A large daily schedule can be posted in front of the room indicating the subject areas to be covered during the day as well as the time allotted for each. This will assist the class in moving from one subject area to the next promptly. Soon it will become routine. The teacher preparing this chart must have these sessions organized to fit in with the regular classes of the high school. At certain times of the day, his class will be operating on the regular bell schedule while at other times his class may be engrossed in a lesson as the classes outside the room are changing. As you will note, some periods are scheduled on a regular basis, while other periods are split to accommodate the needs at this level. It is suggested here to include a copy of your daily schedule in your plan book along with your specific objectives for each subject area for convenience in planning.

Your attention is now directed to Table III, which illustrates a sample daily schedule.

For additional classroom organization, it is advisable to get into the habit of using a standard heading on all papers for work done in the classroom. The only item that should ever change is the subject area, and this area should be indicated in the upper right-hand corner. Other items might include student's name, date, and the room number.

Teacher-made materials distributed to the students should also have the standard heading, with a blank space for the student's name. These papers should have holes punched before distribu-

TABLE III
DAILY SCHEDULE

Period	Regular High School Hours	Monday		Tuesday		Wednesday		Thursday		Friday	
	7:55- 8:05	OPENING EXERCISES									
1	8:09- 8:49	Arith.	R	Shop (Boys) Home Ec. (Girls)	R	Reading	R	Health	R	Shop (Boys) Home Ec. (Girls)	R
2	8:53- 9:33	Spelling	R	Science	R	Social Studies	R	Phys. Ed.	R	Reading	R
3	9:37-10:17	Social Studies	R	Reading	R	Art	R	Comp. 9:37 / 9:57; Science 9:59 / 10:17	S	Spelling 9:37 / 9:57; Arith. 9:59 / 10:17	S
4	10:21-11:01	Music	R	Comp.	R	Comp. 10:21 / 10:41; Pen. 10:43 / 11:01	S	Spelling 10:21 / 10:41; Social Studies 10:43 / 11:01	S	Citizen.	R
	11:01-11:30	STUDENT'S LUNCH PERIOD—DEPART FOR WORK*									
5	11:35-12:15	TEACHER-COORDINATOR'S LUNCH									
6	12:19-12:59	TEACHER-COORDINATOR'S TIME FOR SUPERVISION AND COORDINATING PROGRAM									
7	1:03- 1:43										
8	1:47- 2:27	Citizen.	R	Health**	R	Arith.**	R	Citizen. 1:47 / 2:07; Pen. 2:09 / 2:27	S	Work Study; Seminar	R

R = Regular Period
S = Split Period

*Some students eat lunch at work.

**Every other week these periods scheduled for shop & cooking activities.

tion. In this connection, each student should have at least two, three-ring notebooks for filing materials under specific subject areas. Admittedly, it takes time to get the students into this routine but, once they are underway, they will soon develop a real sense of pride in being organized for instruction. In a sense, you are constantly developing good housekeeping habits in your curriculum. You will also talk occasionally about the safekeeping of important papers such as social security cards, birth certificates, and tax forms. One way you can start developing good-housekeeping habits in the classroom is to list on the board some criteria for maintaining a good notebook and then to go from student to student, presenting constructive suggestions and assigning a grade for a job well done. For a bell-work activity, have one of the students distribute papers you have examined or marked for filing. Assign faster students to assist the slower ones in this task. Keep in mind, our students at this level want to be like the regular students at the high school level. Here is an opportunity for them to do so. In this respect, individuals are sometimes embarrassed to carry with them on the school bus certain texts and materials representing elementary achievement levels. This is natural and can be expected. The answer here is to acquire the more sophisticated materials geared for these youth. You can also secure some attractive book covers for all of their books.

As far as the classroom is concerned, you and I know that the best place to operate the program is in neat and attractive surroundings. Every item in the classroom has a place. You will build up an inventory of many materials and aids you may have tested. Have the students build a chart rack for stowing these materials. If you make your charts standard size, this is no problem and they will be easy to locate when you start reviewing various areas covered during the year. Build a small wooden filing cubicle to store all your dittos by subject area. Making this cubicle provides an excellent project for the shop class. Occasionally, it is advisable to conduct a general cleanup. Have certain students assigned to various areas in the class. Rotate the assignments. Have a student make a daily check on the materials stowed in individual students' desks. Make neatness a factor in the room. You as the teacher set the pattern in good housekeeping, and this positive trait will be hopefully assimilated by your students.

Moreover, take full advantage of the bulletin boards in your room. They have an important place in the learning process as well as in making your room attractive. Use your main board for the current units you are exploring. On top of the chalkboard, you might want to incorporate the *work tip* for the week. Examples could include

"Leave home early for work in bad weather."

"The dependable worker is on time every day."

"Don't get into the habit of taking days off."

You can develop many of these tips from your objectives. Use large print on heavy manila paper and make the posters standard size. Soon you will build up a collection for future use.

On other bulletin board areas, provide good grooming tips, general safety rules for working, qualities of the good worker, and current notices. Later, you might post photographs of your students on various jobs for all to see what various occupational areas are being explored in the program. A Polaroid™ camera would be a luxury item for the work study program, but you could certainly put one to excellent use in the classroom, especially when you start correlating instruction with the work phase of the program. For example, Tom has been placed recently on a new work training site. This particular company has an industrial-type time clock with a clock face unlike the ones to which the class has been accustomed. Where the numbers 12, 3, 6, and 9 would be indicated, this particular clock has two vertical and horizontal markings. In any event, this setup has provided some confusion to Tom when he punches in and out for work. To remedy this problem for Tom and to capitalize on this as a learning experience for the entire class, the teacher-coordinator takes these steps: In his supervisory rounds to keep in touch with Tom and his employer, the instructor takes a picture of the clock. He brings the photograph back to class and, with the assistance of an opaque projector, presents the problem to the class. With this approach, the students have some point of reference knowing that one of their own classmates encountered this problem. Hopefully, it might provide them with a realistic reason for learning that time clocks may have a variety of clock faces which the students must be prepared to cope with in the future. There are many other innovative ways the alert teacher can capitalize on real work experience and problems as learning experiences for his group. This can be accomplished more readily in a classroom that is well organized for program instruction.

Discussion Problems and Activities

1. List the areas of information which an up-to-date individual cumulative record folder might contain.
2. Discuss the ways you might integrate your students with the regular students at the high school.
3. Other than occupational goals on the part of the parents, what information might be helpful to gather at a home visit?
4. Discuss whether the teacher-coordinator should join a service group in the community in which he teaches.
5. Locate various screening procedures used for admission to the school work study programs. What seem to be the common factors in each?
6. Keeping in mind the physical difference in the chronological age range served and the great need for individual student storage space for books and materials, what kinds of desks would you order for the work study program?
7. List the additional science materials and equipment you would order for the science table for the work study program. What kinds of tools would you need for your in-class shop program?
8. Discuss the ways you might justify the need of an outside telephone for your program.
9. Discuss the advantages and disadvantages of having the students' individual lockers located close to the classroom itself.
10. List the specific objectives you could meet quite readily in various subjects if you had an industrial-type time clock in your room.
11. Make a list of twenty-five work tips that could be used for the "work tip of the week" aspect of your program.

12. Devise five constructive bell-work activities that could be used in the work study program.
13. What advantage to the teacher-coordinator is offered by scheduling his science period immediately after the period when his class is at gym or art?
14. Discuss the pro's and con's regarding homework for the students participating in the work study program?
15. Make a list of the areas you would want to discuss with your students on the opening day of school.

Chapter IV

DEVELOPING YOUR PROGRAM

In the process of developing your program, you will be concerned with many areas. Three of the areas requiring your immediate attention will be discussed in this chapter. Examine the suggestions provided below for developing an effective record system, for developing a "school-public information" plan, and for setting up a system to interview prospective employers.

Developing a Record System

The importance of an efficient record-keeping system is obvious to all. Many times the teacher-coordinator must have information at his fingertips. He cannot afford to spend time searching through his files for information when he has a busy employer or a school administrator waiting on the telephone. He must have the answers or know where to locate them quickly. Organization in this respect will make the total job less demanding, and the program will operate that much smoother.

Like the special class teachers at other levels who have their share of record-keeping duties—attendance records, report cards, anecdotal records, and inventories, to name a few—the instructor of the work study program will be concerned with these duties plus other record-keeping tasks in conjunction with his program. At this point, let us consider organizing and developing an effective system to get you underway.

Start with a standard-size filing cabinet with four drawers. This cabinet will contain certain confidential information regarding your students. It is mandatory that it include a lock for security reasons. Acquire two boxes of regular-size file folders and you are ready to begin.

Take the four drawers, organize your record and filing system into four major areas, and assign various section headings as below:

1. Work Study Program Forms (*Section A*)
2. Student Records and Related Information (*Section B*)
3. Work Study Aids, Correspondence, and Completed Reports (*Section C*)
4. General Program Operations (*Section D*)

In the future, you might want to subdivide these sections as you enlarge particular areas. Now let us provide some possible suggestions for subgrouping these various sections. (After having your program in operation for a few years, you may wish to devise your own system.)

Work Study Program Forms
(Section A)

1. Work Study Assignment Lists*
2. Work Assignment Transportation and Time Schedules*
3. Work Study Progress Reports*
4. Work Study Progress Cumulative Reports*
5. Teacher-coordinator Daily Program Schedules*
6. Student Physical Check Forms*
7. Work Certificates Check Forms*
8. Work Certificate Applications Forms
9. Student Birth Certification Copy Forms*
10. Pre-vocational Skills Forms
11. Job Interview Forms
12. Job Analysis Schedule Forms
13. Job Physical Capacities Forms
14. Student Job Placement Information Forms*
15. Handicapped Worker Applications for Certificate (State)
16. Handicapped Worker Applications for Certificate (Federal)
17. Work Study Program Summary Forms*
18. Student Termination from Work Study Program Forms
19. Job Training Lead Forms*
20. Accident Report Forms
21. Employee's Withholding Exemption Certificates (W-4 forms)
22. Federal and State Tax Forms
23. Teacher-coordinator Mileage Forms
24. Payroll List Forms*
25. Payroll Accounting Forms*
26. Individual Pay-Time Record Forms*
27. Employment Application Forms
28. Teacher-coordinator Time Schedule Forms*
   *Copy of each included in this book.

Student Records and Related Information
(Section B)

1. Students' Permanent Record Cards
2. Medical Reports and Records

3. Attendance Information
4. Absent and Tardy Excuses
5. Parent Requests (notes)
6. Letters from Parents
7. Student Work Progress Reports (completed)
8. Student Work Record Forms (completed)
9. Employment Certificates (current)
10. Employment Certificates (copies)
11. Birth Certificates (copies)
12. Pre-vocational Skills Forms (completed)
13. State Handicapped Worker Applications (completed)
14. State Handicapped Worker Certificates Issued
15. Student Work Time Records
16. Federal Handicapped Worker Applications (completed)
17. Federal Handicapped Worker Certificates Issued
18. Student Reference Letters
19. Student Anecdotal Notes for Filing
20. Vocational Evaluations
21. Individual Pay and Time Record Forms
22. Individual Student Cumulative Record Folders

Work Study Aids, Correspondence, and Completed Forms
(Section C)

1. Federal Labor Laws
2. State Labor Laws
3. Service Groups
4. Community Agencies
5. Work Training Aids
6. Vocational Education Information
7. State Employment Office Information
8. State Division of Vocational Rehabilitation Information
9. Community Information
10. Work Preparation Aids
11. Training Programs and Projects
12. Federal and State Wage Information
13. Workmen's Compensation Information
14. Social Security Information
15. Accident Report File
16. Insurance Information
17. Public Information Folder
18. Labor Unions Information
19. Work Study Parent Information
20. Work Study Program Literature
21. Work Study Budget
22. Follow-up Information
23. Work Study Problems
24. Work Assignment Lists*
25. Work Assignment Time and Transportation Schedules*
26. Work Study Progress Cumulative Reports*
27. Work Certificates Check Forms*
28. Work Certificates*
29. Job Analysis Schedules*
30. Job Interview Forms*
31. Job Physical Capacities Forms*
32. Work Study Summary Forms*
33. Termination from Work Study Program Forms*
34. Payroll Lists*
35. Individual Payroll Records*
36. Payroll Balance Sheets*
37. List of Employers (business, industry, school)
38. Teacher-coordinator Time Schedules*

*Completed copies of.

General Program Operations
(Section D)

1. School Policies
2. Curriculum Aides
3. Curriculum Guide
4. Curriculum Overview
5. Meetings and Conferences
6. Text Inventories
7. Equipment Inventories
8. Library Book Inventories
9. Supplies and Materials Catalogs
10. Film Catalogs
11. Professional Literature File
12. Requisitions
13. Education Laws
14. Clippings
15. Bibliographies

In developing your filing system, you might type an index of all the folders contained in each section and tape it to the outside of the drawer for quick reference.

Assign a number to each folder. Be sure that the numbers correspond to the index, and stagger your folder tab-headings for easier retrieval.

At your desk, you might include a copy of all outgoing correspondence that you initiate during the school year. This is easily done by making an extra carbon copy of each letter. This will provide a convenient check system to letters requesting a reply. When you receive the answer, you can make a notation at the bottom of the copy regarding date received and where you filed the reply. At the end of the school year, you can file the correspondence that you have originated in respective folders.

For more effective filing procedures, you can easily assign serial numbers to your correspondence. Each of the four major groupings was just assigned a section letter: A, B, C, and D. Section C was your file drawer on Work Study Aids, Correspondence, and Completed Reports. For example, if you sent a letter of request to the local Social Security Administration (Folder No. 14) for materials, you could serialize the letter as C/14. Agreed, it is a little extra effort to get your record system started but, in long run, it will provide your program with real dividends in time saved.

At your desk, consider the investment of a 3-by-5-inch card file and the necessary cards for setting up a ready reference to your program. The first section might include a card for each of your students participating in the program. A duplicate of the registration card the students fill out the first day of school would be sufficient for this; however, include their social security numbers and their locker numbers and combinations. The second section might include individual cards on all work experience sites. Include supervisor's name, manager, building principal, telephone number, and mailing address. The third section might include work training site placements. Here, you want basically the same information as for the work exjerience section, but include the name of the current student undergoing training. The fourth section might list work training sites where there are openings, with the information similar to the above sections. In the fifth section, you might include a card of all students who have left your program for various reasons. In the future, some excellent follow-up data for your program might be thus provided.

You will agree that an appointment schedule and a telephone index are absolute essentials. Keep a note pad always available on your desk for anecdotal notes on your students and for getting all details over the phone when a problem arises concerning your program.

Developing a "School-Public Information" Plan

As previously indicated, the school work study program needs the cooperation of many people. We have continually referred to the program as *your* program, more in a sense of pride and in the responsibility the job entails than in a possessive sense. But, the ultimate success of the program rests with the cooperative efforts of the numerous people involved. To be truly involved, they must be aware of what exists and why it exists. Equally important, they must be familiar with the part they must play in its operation. To do this, the teacher-coordinator must publicize the program with a perennial selling campaign.

At this point, the Board of Education, the Pupil Personnel Services, the various school administrators, supervisors, directors, and the other teacher-coordinators of the regular work study programs are aware of your program's needs. You have their support. However, there are others you must sell. Who are these individuals? How is this done?

In answer to the first question, consider the following groups of individuals to be reached with this plan:
1. The high school student body.
2. Fellow high school teachers
3. School-wide nonprofessional employees (custodians, cafeteria workers, bus drivers, office workers)
4. The parents
5. Members of the community (industry, business, service, civic and church groups)

These people are reached in a variety of ways and in various phases of timing. Let us begin with the first phase. This part will coincide with the work experience phase, where you will be preparing your students for initial placement within the various in-school jobs. Weigh these suggestions:

Phase I (possibly first 10 weeks of school)
1. Start with a series of articles in the school newspaper. Include an introduction. Why this program? Chart the program's progress.
2. Follow up these articles with a short talk at an assembly program. Describe how the regular students can aid the program. State the value of the program to your students.
3. Secure ten minutes for a short presentation at one of your faculty meetings. Discuss the learning characteristics of your group. Have teachers reinforce with their students what you have discussed in the assembly program.
4. Meet with your fellow special class teachers to organize a meeting for all parents of special class youngsters concerning "our" school work study program plans. Discuss the agenda.

Phase II (next 10 weeks of school)
1. Develop a brochure for parents. Use about five pages explaining your program.[15] Include these areas:
   Why the program? Introduction letter by the principal.
   People in school to contact (phone numbers).
   Copy of the daily schedule.
   Length of the course and areas to be covered.
   Requirements for a certificate.
   Typical high school day.
   Brief description of the program.
   Questions of interest.

General school information (lockers, supplies, cafeteria) .
Parent-conference schedule and record.

2. Schedule the parent meeting at your room. Discuss the program and distribute the brochure. Stress that parental cooperation is needed.

3. Secure ten minutes at the next school employees' meeting. This group usually meets monthly. State specifically how they can help the program. Give them some tips in working with your group.

4. Deliver a short article and a photograph of your group to the community newspaper showing your class members receiving their first pay checks.

Phase III (third 10 weeks of school)

1. Make slides of your program to date. Include steps in its organization, the work experience phase to date. Show the slides at your first *open-house.*

2. Have your students prepare refreshments for an after-school meeting with representatives from your staff and your local Division of Vocational Rehabilitation counselor, a supervisor from the local rehabilitation center and/or sheltered workshop, a representative from your local state employment office, and your building principal. Discuss your program. Tell where you are headed. Incorporate suggestions offered by these persons and note the assistance they can provide.

3. Schedule a few speaking engagements in the community with local church and civic groups. Briefly describe your program; show your slides; indicate the forthcoming assistance you will be needing for your work training phase.

4. Develop an informative bulletin board for your room showing students on various jobs and progress made in the program. Call a parent meeting and pinpoint various trouble areas where parents can be of assistance.

5. Deliver a photograph to the local community newspaper showing a group of your students opening savings accounts at the local bank.

Phase IV (last 10 weeks of school)

1. Determine what students will be ready for out-of-school job placement next year and what specific training areas you are

seeking. Send letters to local personnel managers including a brief description of the program. Request an appointment.

2. Schedule and present a program for the local service groups. Tell them what you are doing in your program. Describe what the students are doing and how the service groups can assist the program regarding training sites.

3. Present your outstanding worker awards at the end-of-the-year awards assembly. Consider these awards: Most Improved Worker, Worker of the Year, and Most Dependable Worker.

Aside from the suggestions just given in the four-phase plan for making your program known, you will have your own ideas to incorporate during the program's first year of operation. However, the suggestions provided may give you a point of reference to begin your thinking in connection with an effective "school-public information" plan.

Developing a System to Interview Prospective Employers

In conjunction with your "school-public information" plan, you must be prepared to follow through on various work training leads for your program. This phase will depend upon the philosophy underlining your program. Do you procure a training site first, then select the student to fill this job in accordance with his aptitudes, potential, and desire? Or, do you first evaluate the skills of the individual student and then set out to procure a compatible training site to accommodate this student? Or, do you incorporate a combination of both in your program? These are questions that should be considered. Naturally, the community where the program is located may dictate the answer to these questions, as well as the current employment situation. In any event, be prepared with an effective system for interviewing prospective employers.

Whether you send out letters briefly introducing your program beforehand or not, always make it a policy to write or telephone ahead requesting an appointment. This is the proper way to do business for obvious reasons. At the interview, be ready to explain your program. You might prepare a description of your program to assist you. Describe how the program is organized, particular selling points about your students, and the assistance you can provide during the training phase. Show some pictures of your students in the work experience phase. Point out how well-groomed they are and emphasize the time you spend on developing important work qualities in the classroom.

In addition to being well-prepared for the selling aspect of the interview, learn as much as you can about the company beforehand. Locate someone in the community who is employed there and, over an informal cup of coffee, you can gain a perspective of this particular company as seen by a member of the labor force.

At the interview with the management, however, stick to the point. Be brief, but do not rush to end the meeting if the personnel manager is still eager to give or receive information.[37] It would be wise to have with you a form you have developed to record the information acquired at the interview. Consider the following information[37]:

1. Payroll title
2. Dictionary of Occupational Titles Code Number
3. Name of company
4. Employer
5. Address
6. Phone
7. Person responsible for hiring
8. Person responsible for training
9. Number of employees
10. Name of union
11. Beginning hourly rate
12. Physical requirements
13. Required tools
14. Labor turnover

In the event that there is a training site open and the personnel manager would like to cooperate with your program, be prepared to get the specifics of the job.

The U.S. Department of Labor has available for a small charge an excellent *Training and Reference Manual for Job Analysis*[38] that will aid you considerably in this respect.

On the other hand, if you cannot get a definite commitment at this time, discuss the possibility of a probationary period for one of your students on a trial basis. If the personnel manager would like some time to contemplate his decision, attach your business card to the program description sheet and gain his permission to call him back in a few days.

Discussion Problems and Activities

1. Outline a letter you might wish to send to a personnel manager briefly describing your program.
2. Who has the responsibility for making out the accident report on a student worker in school?
3. Why should you keep copies of students' excuses on file?
4. What serial numbers would you give these letters: a letter to a student's family physician, a letter of reference for an ex-student, a letter to the Rotary Club?
5. Discuss where you might be able to get secretarial assistance for your program within the school.
6. List some other points you might want to get across to teachers at a faculty meeting regarding your program.
7. Discuss some probable questions you might field at the first parents' meeting.
8. Would you consider in your talk to the school employees defining the difference between *mental illness* and *mental retardation?*
9. What method of communication would you use to contact parents who did not attend a scheduled parents' meeting?
10. Make a list of ways parents can help your work study program.
11. Discuss and record questions the personnel manager might ask you regarding the school work study program.
12. Discuss this question: "Should the term *educable mentally retarded* be included on your program's business card?"
13. If you get the opportunity to tour the plant while at the interview, what will you be prepared to look for?
14. In gaining background information on a company, what information would be helpful to you from a local employee?

Chapter V

OPERATING YOUR PROGRAM

This chapter will brief you on some of the legal requirements and certain employment limitations regarding your student workers. Later, we will explore the possibilities of developing a balance of time for you to accomplish your many duties.

Legal Requirements and Employment Limitations

For the protection of your students, your school system, and yourself, it would be wise to become knowledgeable in this area as soon as possible. In doing so, you will become aware that there are two distinct categories of laws which will affect your program. These include *state* and *federal* Child Labor Laws.

Briefly, every *state* has Child Labor Laws.[35] They follow well-defined patterns, but they vary widely in the various standards which are set up for the employment of boys and girls. The range of occupations which they include also differs from state to state. Standards for the following areas would be included[35]:

1. Minimum wage
2. Employment certificates
3. Hours of work
4. Hazardous occupations

Also, review the compulsory school attendance requirements in your state. Your attention is directed to Tables IV, V, VI, and VII, which provide a summary (by states) of the minimum ages for employment. In reviewing these tables, keep in mind that not all exemptions are shown. A few states set a lower employment age for minors found to be incapable of profiting from continuing school attendance.[35]

TABLE IV*

MINIMUM AGE FOR EMPLOYMENT IN MANUFACTURING OCCUPATIONS
OR ESTABLISHMENTS UNDER STATE CHILD LABOR LAWS

16 Years .... 20 States

Alabama	Kentucky	Montana	Rhode Island
Alaska[1]	Louisiana	New Jersey	South Carolina
Colorado[2]	Maine	New York	Tennessee
Connecticut	Maryland[3]	North Carolina	Virginia[3]
Georgia[1]	Massachusetts	Pennsylvania	West Virginia[4]

15 Years .... 1 State

Texas

14 Years .... 28 States, the
District of Columbia
and Puerto Rico

Arizona	Indiana	Oklahoma
Arkansas[1]	Iowa[1]	Oregon[5]
California (15 during school hours except 14 if 8th grade completed and work necessary for family support) [5]	Kansas Michigan[1] [2] Minnesota Mississippi[3] Missouri[1]	Puerto Rico (16 during hours) [7] South Dakota[8] Utah Vermont[2]
Delaware[5]	Nebraska	Washington (14 for boys, 16
District of Columbia	Nevada[6]	for girls) [7]
Hawaii (16 when legally required to attend school) [1]	New Hampshire[1] New Mexico[6]	Wisconsin (16 during school hours)
Idaho[5]	North Dakota	Wyoming (16 during school
Illinois (16 during school hours)	Ohio (16 during school hours) [4]	hours)

12 Years .... 1 State

Florida (16 during school hours, *except* 12 if legally excused from school attendance, 12 outside school hours) [2]

50 States, the
District of Columbia
and Puerto Rico

[1]Specific parental exemption: *In an occupation or business owned, controlled, or operated by parent:* Alaska, Iowa, and Michigan, and during vacations only in Arkansas. *In an employment by or service for parent:* Georgia, Missouri, and New Hampshire, and in Hawaii in nonhazardous work when the child is not legally required to attend school.

[2]In *Colorado,* the Industrial Commission may grant special exemptions in individual cases if it finds it is in minor's best interest. In *Florida,* the Industrial Commission may suspend the provisions of the child labor law in individual cases if it is necessary for a minor 12 and over to support himself or his family or if it is recommended by the juvenile court that such employment is for the minor's best interest. In *Michigan,* the Industrial Commission is authorized to make deviations "whenever

necessary in the interests of the general public or the individual minor." In *Vermont,* the Commissioner of Industrial Relations may exempt from the child labor law, for 2 months a year, a manufacturing establishment whose products are perishable.

[3]Lower minimum age or no minimum age in canneries: Mississippi; in community noncommercial packing or canning establishments in Maryland and Virginia.

[4]High-school graduates exempted from 16-year minimum in Ohio. Those completing highest grade available exempted in West Virginia and Wisconsin.

[5]Lower minimum age permitted for work outside school hours and during vacations: Arizona, California, Delaware (boys), Idaho, Oregon.

[6]No minimum age outside school hours or during vacations: Nevada, New Mexico.

[7]In *Puerto Rico,* under certain conditions a minor 14 or 15 may be employed during school hours in non-hazardous employment on special certificate. In *Washington,* judges of a superior court may issue permits to boys under 14 and girls under 16 for any inside employment.

[8]*South Dakota*: Employment may be permitted where necessary for the support of the child or his family.

*Courtesy of U.S. Department of Labor, Division of State Services and Standards.

TABLE V

MINIMUM AGE FOR EMPLOYMENT DURING SCHOOL HOURS UNDER STATE CHILD LABOR LAWS**

16-YEAR MINIMUM AGE DURING SCHOOL HOURS IN ANY GAINFUL OCCUPATION OR IN ANY GAINFUL OCCUPATION EXCEPT AGRICULTURE AND DOMESTIC SERVICE ....21 States and Puerto Rico

Any gainful occupation ....10 States and Puerto Rico

Colorado[1] [2]	Maryland[4]	New Jersey	Puerto Rico[6]
Florida[3]	Montana	New York	Virginia[4] [5]
Illinois		Ohio[5]	Wyoming

Any gainful occupation except agriculture and domestic service .... 11 States

Alabama[5] [6]	Louisiana	Rhode Island	West Virginia[5]
Georgia[2] [5]	North Carolina	South Carolina	Wisconsin (only
Kentucky[5]	Pennsylvania	Tennessee[6]	agriculture exempted) [5]

16-YEAR MINIMUM AGE DURING SCHOOL HOURS IN SPECIFIED ESTABLISHMENTS OR INDUSTRIES .... 4 States

Alaska[2]	Connecticut[4]	Maine[7]	Massachusetts[6]

16-YEAR MINIMUM AGE WHEN LEGALLY REQUIRED TO ATTEND SCHOOL, 14 WHEN NOT LEGALLY REQUIRED TO ATTEND SCHOOL .... 1 State

Any gainful occupation except domestic service
Hawaii[8]

15-YEAR MINIMUM AGE DURING SCHOOL HOURS .... 2 States

Any gainful occupation .... 1 State

California[9]

Specified establishments only .... 1 State
Texas

14-YEAR MINIMUM AGE DURING SCHOOL HOURS .... 22 States and the District of Columbia

Any gainful occupation ....14 States and D.C.

Arizona	Idaho	Missouri[2]	North Dakota
Arkansas	Indiana	Nebraska	Oregon
District of	Kansas	Nevada	Utah[2]
Columbia	Minnesota	New Mexico	Vermont[10]

Any gainful occupation except agriculture and domestic service ....4 States

Delaware	Washington (but 16 for girls in
Michigan[2] [10]	certain occupations) [6]
New Hampshire[2]	

Specified establishments only ....4 States

Iowa[2]	Mississippi	Oklahoma	South Dakota[14]

50 States, the
District of Columbia,
and Puerto Rico

[1] In *Colorado,* a child of 14 may be employed in nonhazardous work during school hours if legally excused from school attendance, and a child 14 participating in a school-work or supervised educational activity is exempt from all provisions of the child labor law except the hazardous provisions. In addition, the Industrial Commission may grant special exemptions in individual cases from any provision of the act if it finds it in the best interest of the child involved.

[2] Specific parental exemption: *Nonfactory work done for a parent, unless parent receives payment therefor*—Colorado. *In business owned or operated by parent*—Alaska, Iowa. *Employed by parent*—Georgia, Missouri, New Hampshire, Utah. *In a trade in which parent is self-employed*—Michigan.

[3] In *Florida,* a child of 12 may be employed during school hours if legally excused from school attendance. In addition, the Industrial Commission may suspend any provision of the child labor law for non-hazardous work in individual cases if it is necessary for a minor 12 and over to support himself or his family or if it is recommended by the juvenile court that such employment is for minor's best interest.

[4] *Connecticut, Maryland,* and *Virginia* exempt children 14 or over participating in a school-work program.

[5] High school graduates exempted in any employment in Ohio; in nonfactory employment in Alabama, Georgia, Kentucky, and Virginia. Those completing the highest grade available are exempted in West Virginia and Wisconsin.

[6] In *Alabama,* minors of 14 and 15 may be employed in nonhazardous work when school attendance has been waived. In *Massachusetts,* minors 14 may be employed in nonfactory or nonmechanical establishments if for child's welfare. In *Puerto Rico,* under certain conditions, a special certificate may be issued for children 14 and 15 in occupations determined nonhazardous by the Secretary of Labor. In *Tennessee,* minors under 16 may be employed in nonfactory work if excused from school attendance. In *Washington,* judges of a superior court may issue permits to boys under 14 and girls under 16 for any inside employment.

[7] *Maine:* Specified employments include manufacturing and mechanical establishments. Other employments prohibited during school hours for minors under 14 and under 15, with parental exemptions.

[8] In *Hawaii,* minors 10 to 14 when not legally required to attend school may work for an employer in the coffee-growing industry after the Director has determined that sufficient adult labor is not available.

[9] In *California,* a 14-year minimum age applies if the 8th grade is completed and the minor's earnings are needed for family support.

[10] In *Michigan,* the Industrial Commissioner is authorized to make deviations "whenever necessary in the interest of the general public or the individual minor." In *Vermont,* the Commissioner of Industrial Relations may exempt from the child labor law, for 2 months a year, a manufacturing establishment whose products are perishable.

11 In *South Dakota,* employment may be permitted under 14 during certain hours where necessary for the support of the child or his family.

* Courtesy of U.S. Department of Labor, Division of States Services and Standards.

** This table does not include compulsory school attendance requirements.

TABLE VI*

MINIMUM AGE OUTSIDE SCHOOL HOURS IN FACTORIES
AND STORES UNDER STATE CHILD LABOR LAWS**

16 IN FACTORIES AND STORES .... 1 State
   Connecticut

16 IN FACTORIES, 14 IN STORES .... 17 States

Alabama[1]	Kentucky	North Carolina
Alaska[2]	Louisiana	Pennsylvania
Colorado[2, 3]	Maine[2]	Rhode Island
Georgia (12 for boys in	Maryland	Tennessee
wholesale or retail	Massachusetts	Virginia
stores) [2]	New Jersey	West Virginia (16 for girls
	New York	in stores) [4]

16 IN FACTORIES; NO MINIMUM IN STORES .... 2 States
   Montana   South Carolina

15 IN FACTORIES; NO MINIMUM IN STORES .... 1 State
   Texas

14 IN FACTORIES AND STORES .... 22 States, the
                                              District of Columbia,
                                              and Puerto Rico

Arizona[1]	Indiana	North Dakota
Arkansas[2]	Iowa[2]	Ohio
California[1]	Kansas	Oregon[1]
Delaware[1]	Michigan[2, 3]	Puerto Rico
District of Columbia	Mississippi	Utah
Hawaii[2]	Missouri[2]	Washington (but 16 for
Idaho[1]	Nebraska	girls) [5]
Illinois	New Hampshire[2]	Wisconsin
		Wyoming

14 IN FACTORIES; NO MINIMUM IN STORES .... 4 States

Minnesota	South Dakota[6]	Vermont[3]
Oklahoma		

12 IN FACTORIES AND STORES .... 1 State
   Florida

NO MINIMUM AGE OUTSIDE SCHOOL HOURS .... 2 States

Nevada	New Mexico

                                              50 States, the
                                              District of Columbia,
                                              and Puerto Rico

[1] Lower minimum age during school vacation periods or weekly school holidays: Alabama in stores only (boys 12), Arizona (boys 10), California (12), Delaware (boys 12), Idaho (12), Oregon (12).

[2] Specific parental exemption: *In business owned and operated by parent*—Alaska, Iowa, and Michigan. *Employed by parent*—Arkansas, Colorado (in nonfactory work unless parent receives payment therefor), Georgia, Hawaii (in nonhazardous work) Maine (applies to stores but not to factories), Missouri, New Hampshire.

3 Special exemptions: Colorado—The Industrial Commissioner may grant a special exemption if he finds that it is for minor's best interest. Michigan—The Commissioner of Labor is authorized to make deviations "whenever necessary in the interest of the general public or the individual minor." Vermont—The Commissioner of Industrial Relations may exempt from the child labor law, for 2 months a year, a manufacturing establishment whose products are perishable.

4 West Virginia: Graduate of highest grade available.

5 Washington: Judges of a superior court may issue permits to boys under 14 and girls under 16 for any inside employment.

6 South Dakota: Employment may be permitted under 14 where it is necessary for the support of the child or his family.

*Courtesy of U.S. Department of Labor, Division of State Services and Standards.

**In some cases, the ages given apply to other establishments also, in addition to factories and stores.

TABLE VII*

MINIMUM AGE FOR EMPLOYMENT IN AGRICULTURE UNDER STATE CHILD LABOR LAWS

State	During school hours	Outside school hours and during school vacations
I. Agriculture Covered[1]		20 States, the District of Columbia, and Puerto Rico
Alaska	No minimum age[2]	14[3]
California	15[4]	14[3, 4]
Colorado	16[3, 5]	12[3]
Connecticut	14	14[6]
District of Columbia	14	14[3]
Florida	16[7]	No minimum age.
Hawaii	16 when a child is "required" to attend school, otherwise 14.[3]	14[3, 8]
Illinois	16	No minimum age.
Indiana	14	No minimum age.
Maryland	16	No minimum age.
Massachusetts	14	No minimum age.
Minnesota	14	No minimum age.
Missouri	14[3]	14[3]
New Jersey	16	12[3]
New York	16	14[3, 9]
Ohio	16	No minimum age.
Pennsylvania	15 (14 under certain conditions).	No minimum age.
Puerto Rico	16[10]	14
Texas	14[3]	14[3, 11]
Utah	14[3]	10[3]
Virginia	16	No minimum age if work is with consent of child's parent (otherwise 14).
Wisconsin	12[3]	12[3, 12]

II. General Minimum Age Standard Might Be Interpreted To Cover Agriculture .... 13 States

Arizona	14	No minimum age.
Arkansas	14	14[3]
Idaho	14	No minimum age.

Kansas............................. 14..............................	No minimum age.
Maine.............................. 15³.............................	No minimum age.
Montana.......................... 16..............................	No minimum age.
Nebraska......................... 14..............................	No minimum age.
Nevada............................ 14..............................	No minimum age.
New Mexico..................... 14..............................	No minimum age.
North Dakota.................. 14..............................	No minimum age.
Oregon............................ 14..............................	No minimum age.
Vermont.......................... 14..............................	No minimum age.
Wyoming......................... 16 (enrolled in school)	No minimum age.

III. NO MINIMUM AGE IN AGRICULTURE EITHER DURING OR
OUTSIDE SCHOOL HOURS .... 17 States

Alabama	Louisiana	North Carolina	South Dakota
Delaware	Michigan	Oklahoma	Tennessee
Georgia	Mississippi	Rhode Island	Washington
Iowa	New Hampshire	South Carolina	West Virginia
Kentucky			

50 States, the
District of Columbia,
and Puerto Rico

1 Coverage indicated by express language, by implication, or by legislative history.

2 Alaska: However, the school attendance law requires school attendance up to 16 years of age except for those who have completed the 8th or the highest grade available.

3 Specific parental exemption: *In business owned or controlled by parents*—Alaska, Arkansas. *For employment by parent*—California, Colorado (unless parent receives payment therefor), the District of Columbia, Hawaii, Maine, Missouri, New Jersey, New York (12), Texas, Utah, and Wisconsin. See also footnotes 6 and 7.

4 However, in California minors 14 and over who have completed the 8th grade or whose earnings are needed for family support may be employed during school hours; minors 12 and over may be employed during school vacations and on weekly school holidays.

5 Colorado: The Industrial Commissioner may grant special exemptions. In addition, a child of 14 or 15 may be employed if legally excused from school attendance.

6 In Connecticut, the law applies only during weeks in which the average number of employees exceeds 15. Members of employer's immediate family are exempt.

7 Florida: A minor under 16 years of age may be employed under the following circumstances: if employed by his parent; if 12 years of age and legally excused from school attendance; if 12 and the Industrial Commission deems such employment necessary because of poverty; or if a juvenile court judge recommends his employment.

8 Hawaii: Minors 10 to 14 when not legally required to attend school may work for an employer in the coffee-growing industry after the Director has determined that sufficient adult labor is not available.

9 In New York, children 12 and 13 may assist in the handwork harvest of berries, fruits, and vegetables for not more than 4 hours a day between 9 a.m. and 4 p.m. when school is not in session if such children are accompanied by a parent or have the parent's consent.

10 In Puerto Rico, under certain conditions, a special certificate may be issued for children 14 and 15 in occupations determined nonhazardous by the Secretary of Labor.

11 Texas: No minmum age during June, July, and August.

12 In Wisconsin, an Industrial Commission Order specifies that no minor under 12 may be employed or permitted to work in cherry orchards, market gardening, gardening conducted or controlled by canning companies, and the culture of sugarbeets and cranberries.

*Courtesy of U.S. Department of Labor, Division of State Services and Standards.

In addition to the various state laws, there are three significant *federal* laws having Child Labor Provisions. These laws apply uniformly throughout the country and would include the following:

The Fair Labor Standards Act of 1938, as amended[32]

This Act establishes minimum wage, maximum hours, overtime pay, equal pay and child labor standards for covered employment, unless a specific exemption applies. Effective February 1, 1967, the Fair Labor Standards Amendments of 1966 extended the Act's coverage to more workers and increased the minimum wage for employment already subject to law. Before the amendments the act applied, as it still applies, to employees individually engaged in interstate- or foreign commerce or in the production of goods for such commerce and to employees in certain large enterprises.

The 1966 Amendments' extension of coverage was achieved through the broadening of the definition of a covered enterprise. Also, some exemptions were revised or eliminated.

Among other changes, more retail and service enterprises were brought under the Act. For the first time, the law's standards were extended, in whole or in part, to employees in certain hotels, motels, and restaurants, in hospitals and nursing homes, and in schools. Certain farmworkers were made subject to the minimum wage requirements.

The Walsh-Healy Public Contracts Act[31]

This Act applies to manufacturers or dealers contracting to manufacture or supply materials valued in excess of $10,000, for the United States Government. It requires that no boy under 16 and no girl under 18 years of age shall be employed in any work performed under the contract. (Office employees engaged in office work relating generally to the operation of the business and not engaged in or connected with the manufacture or providing of materials, supplies, articles or equipment are not covered by this act.) This act provides a penalty of $10 a day for each day each minor is knowingly employed contrary to the minimum ages of this act.

The Sugar Act of 1948[31]

This Act contains certain provisions with which producers engaged in the production and harvesting of sugar beets or sugarcane must comply in order to obtain maximum benefit payments. These provisions include a minimum age of 14 years for employment and a maximum 8-hour day for children between 14 and 16 years of age. Members of the immediate family of the legal owner of at least 40 percent of the crop at the time the work is performed are exempted from these provisions. During school hours, however, the higher age standard of 16 set by the Fair Labor Standards Act would be controlling.

Particular note should be taken regarding the Fair Labor Standards Amendments of 1966. As briefly indicated previously, these amendments extended coverage of the Act generally to all employees of elementary and secondary schools. These amendments have definite implications for your work experience phase of the school work study program. Your students working in-school job sites, unless they are specifically exempt, must be paid not less than the minimum wage shown in the following schedule[34]:

- $1.15 an hour, beginning February 1, 1968
- $1.30 an hour, beginning February 1, 1969
- $1.45 an hour, beginning February 1, 1970
- $1.60 an hour, beginning February 1, 1971

The teacher-coordinator should also be aware that both federal and state labor offices issue Handicapped Worker Certificates upon application to their respective offices. With this certificate the handicapped *worker* or *trainee* can be hired for less than the minimum wage. For specific information and regulations regarding these certificates, I suggest that you visit or contact your local, state, and federal labor offices.

It is always good practice to check with the person in charge of hiring at the work experience or work training site before student placement. Determine beforehand what laws (state, federal, or both) are in effect. Usually, this information is posted on the employee's bulletin board. Keep in mind, *whenever state standards for employment of children and federal standards differ, the higher standard is the one that must be observed.* For example, you placed a student in a work training situation at a federal installation and he was going to be employed at the minimum wage. The federal minimum wage might be $1.40 an hour. However, your state minimum wage might be $1.50 an hour. Under law, this student must be paid $1.50 to comply with the higher standard.

It would also be to your advantage to contact federal and state agencies regarding the following important categories with reference to your program[37]:

1. Social security
2. Unemployment insurance

3. Workmen's compensation
4. Disability insurance
5. Hazardous occupations (federal)
6. Taxes
7. Antidiscrimination laws
8. Occupations requiring licensure
9. Prohibited occupations (state)
10. Restrictions to boys and girls under age 18

Budgeting Time for Your Duties

As previously stated, the teacher-coordinator is required to wear many hats in the performance of his duties. Invariably, with a job of this type, it is common practice to become "bogged down" in certain areas of the program, therefore neglecting others equally important. To prevent this, it would be wise to analyze the various roles of the teacher-coordinator and to develop a balance of time for the tasks that must be done. Occasionally, you will have emergency priority items that must be dealt with immediately, but this is usually the exception and not the rule.

To budget your time, some planning and revision in your first few months of operation may be required. Soon it will be done as smoothly as your plan book preparation for the coming week. This can be accomplished effectively if we consider three elements: (1) tasks to be accomplished, (2) time available, and (3) time schedule.

In considering the work-to-be-accomplished area, separate the teaching duties from the coordinating duties which the job demands. Under "teaching," you might include the following tasks to be performed:

1. Instructing
2. Evaluating
3. Correlating
4. Planning
5. Counseling (group)
6. Record-keeping
7. Reporting
8. Selecting
9. Scheduling

10. Preparing

11. Training

Under the "coordinating" aspect of your program, consider the following tasks to be accomplished:

Supervising

Interviewing

Corresponding

Consulting

Surveying

Counseling (individual)

Selling

Reporting

Recommending

Problem-solving

Record-keeping

Conferring

Decision-making

Researching

Next, you must find the time to accomplish these tasks. The classroom instructional schedule will consume at least one-half the school day, including students' lunch period. You must budget your time to take advantage of each minute available during the remainder of the school day. This time could come from free periods you may have while your group is scheduled for special subject areas and/or during your allotted time for supervisory duties in the afternoon. In addition, the time immediately after school, when the students are dismissed, is available. Like all teachers in the profession, you will spend a few evenings of your own time on educational matters. Let us now organize this invaluable commodity and group these various tasks into respective times of the day where they might be accommodated effectively.

As you examine Figures 8, 9, 10, 11, and 12, note that the upper half of each circle is devoted to the instructional phase. The lower half is assigned tasks from the coordinating phase.

Let us briefly summarize what has taken place in our attempt to take full advantage of the time available during the day:

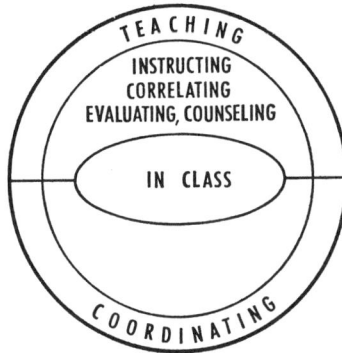

FIG. 8. Teacher-coordinator tasks separated using *in-class* time.

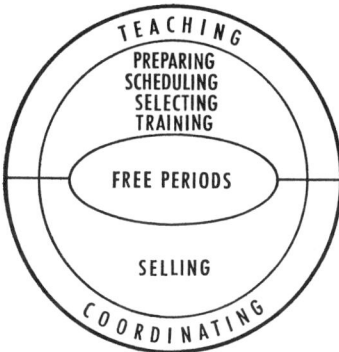

FIG. 9. Teacher-coordinator tasks separated using *free-period* time.

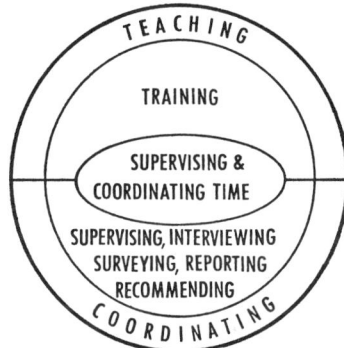

FIG. 10. Teacher-coordinator tasks separated using *supervising and coordinating* time.

FIG. 11. Teacher-coordinator tasks separated using time immediately available *after school.*

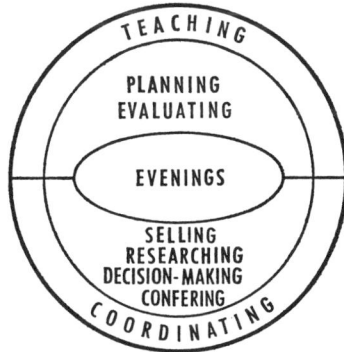

FIG. 12. Teacher-coordinator tasks separated that can be accomplished during *evenings.*

1. We have identified the tasks to be performed.
2. We have separated these tasks by program phases. The program phases would include the instructional and co-ordinating phases.
3. We have grouped them under possible time headings where they might be accommodated during the day.

For example, in Figure 8, the following tasks are indicated: instructing, correlating, evaluating, and counseling. These tasks

Form No. WSP-022

TABLE VIII

TEACHER-COORDINATOR WEEKLY TIME SCHEDULE

Time	Monday Date: 3/12	Tuesday Date: 3/13	Wednesday Date: 3/14	Thursday Date: 3/15	Friday Date: 3/16
Free Periods (9:37-10:17)	*None*	*Prepare correlating materials for social studies lesson on Wednesday.*	*Finish requisitions for next year's supplies.*	*None*	*Review Sect. 3-No. 6, Training Guideline with student Peter Smith.*
Supervising and Coordinating (11:00-1:30)	*Check students at work exp. sites: Junior High Potts Element'y*	*Supervise group departing for work. 12:30— Appointment at Dykes tool company.*	*Check students' progress at work training sites: John Jones Alice Green*	*Prepare Payroll for business office.*	*Report W.S.P.—017 due— Check work exp. site: Palmer Elementary.*
After School (2:30-3:30)	*2:45— Individual counseling session: Al Jackson*	*Start next week's lesson plans.*	*Lesson plans. 3:15 Parent conference, Mrs. Allan.*	*3:00 Special Class teacher's meeting at Palmer Elementary.*	*Letter to: Rotary Club. Complete lesson plans.*
Evenings (7:00-9:00)	*None*	*6:30 P.M.— show film and speak at Kiwanis Club*	*Correct class papers.*	*Lesson plans.*	*Prepare article for school newspaper over weekend.*

are accomplished during the teaching phase. There are no tasks in the coordinating phase in action at this time.

In that we have identified the tasks to be performed, separated these tasks into their respective program phases, grouped them under possible time headings which may be available, let us now examine how they might look on a one-week time-planning schedule. The times indicated in Table VIII are borrowed from the sample daily schedule discussed earlier.

Discussion Problems and Activities

1. What agency issues employment certificates in your community?
2. Visit your local federal and state labor offices and secure the recent publications on Child Labor Laws.
3. Should the teacher at the junior high level have the responsibility of insuring that students leaving his program for the work study program have their social security cards?
4. Would students participating in your program be eligible for disability benefits in your state?
5. Draft a letter to the Wage and Hours and Public Contracts Division, U.S. Department of Labor, requesting Handicapped Worker Applications for your program.
6. Visit your local sheltered workshop director and discuss how Handicapped Worker Certificates are used in his program.
7. What are the hazardous occupations in your state? Are they different from the ones included under the Federal Fair Labor Standards Act?
8. Are students required to pay premiums for workmen's compensation insurance in your state?
9. Prepare yourself to comment on this statement: "I can't hire these youngsters; if they get hurt, my insurance rates will go sky high."
10. In accordance to priority, how would you rank the coordinating phase tasks of the program?
11. Discuss the necessary arrangements that must be made by the teacher-coordinator prior to having a student report for an individual counseling session after school hours.

12. Discuss this statement: "The time available to the teacher-coordinator for coordinating his program really determines the effectiveness of the work study program."

13. What advantage might it present to the teacher-coordinator to keep his weekly time schedules on file for future reference?

14. Prepare a teacher-coordinator time schedule for the month of November. Keep in mind the issuance of report cards during this period.

Chapter VI

CONDUCTING YOUR PROGRAM

At this point, the teacher-coordinator is cognizant of his role as a public relations agent. This role, of course, is expected of all teachers. However, it may be more intensified for you because of the continuous and direct involvement with the many people your program dictates. This section will provide some helpful suggestions to the substitute teacher when you are absent from your post.

Maintaining Effective Relations

If you are by nature a friendly person, the public relations phase of your program will probably come to you naturally.[12] If you are not, you may have to brush up on some basic techniques in this regard. This is an important aspect of your program, and it will be most helpful to you to extend the same courtesies to all you come in contact with as you do your fellow teachers. Being a professional person, you will be expected to conduct your program in a professional manner. In this regard, you are obligated to follow the decisions and policies set by your chief school administrator. Before attempting any major innovations with reference to your program, always clear this through his office via your building principal and supervisor.

Always keep your principal and supervisor up-to-date on the operations of the program. If you have a particular problem worth their attention, contact them immediately for consultation. You will have certain reporting responsibilities; insure that they are accurate and submitted on time. Be sure to get the approval of

65

necessary persons on any news releases you initiate concerning the program. It is wise to maintain effective relations with the person in charge of the school payroll. Develop a line of communication with this person and be prompt with your class payroll list.

As you make your supervisory visits to your in-school job sites, do not hesitate to go out of your way to let your students' employers and fellow employees know that you appreciate their efforts in the habilitating of your young adults. Eventually, you will develop a certain rapport with these individuals that is invaluable. They will gain a sense of pride in their part of the program and on many occasions will inconvenience themselves to bring a certain student along who is having particular difficulty in making his work adjustment. As far as the job managers are concerned, make it a point to consult with them first before you begin the rotation phase of moving students to different jobs. Give them the choice to inform you when it is convenient for them to receive a new employee.

You can do much within the school where you are housed to maintain effective relations with your fellow teachers and regular students. Get involved in the high school program. Previously, it was recommended that you solicit their assistance in your selling campaign. Here is the opportunity for you to become active in some of their activities since many special education teachers assist in school projects or act as advisors for school clubs and many coach varsity sports with great success. Naturally, you will also be involved with your fellow special education teachers and members of the pupil personnel group in a continuous team approach.

Parents have a vital role in your program. It was indicated in your brochure that you have an open-door policy regarding visits to the classroom at any time. This invitation should be extended to include conference time as prearranged. Try to get the parents involved in some of your class projects, outings, and field trips. Keep them informed of the occupational progress of their young adults. Remember, most parents want to help, and they will help if you will let them. Indicate specifically how they can assist the program. Consider the following article with this point in mind:

*Parents Can Help the Work Study Program**

Parents have an important role in the work-study program to help insure that our young adults are adequately prepared to meet the work world with confidence and success. Precisely then, as parents, what can you do?

Start early in your child's education to develop the necessary qualities of a successful worker. Much can be accomplished before your youngster ever enters the work-study phase. Try to have him acquire a sense of responsibility and pride in the job he performs around the home. Strive ardently to have him develop self-control, friendliness, politeness, cooperation, honesty, and punctuality. Supervise closely the way he handles his possessions, or the possessions of other[s]. These are a few of the important qualities that need constant reinforcement. If you are having particular difficulty with a specific area, consult your child's teacher for assistance, but start early.

Likewise, work vigorously on all phases of grooming with your child. Encourage him to develop a sense of neatness in his everyday dress; and as he gets older, and ready for placement in the work program, intensify this training. Here, he will be coming in close contact with fellow employees in various work-experience situations. Emphasize that at the end of each work day a shower and the use of deodorants are a firm requirement.

In conversations at home, try to bring your child into the discussions as frequently as possible. Endeavor to develop interests in our future worker in possible areas in which he can converse with others adequately. Start with small talk, such as the weather, his hobbies, his school lessons, current events, and possibly his chores and duties at home. If Dad or Mom . . . [is a sports fan], get your child involved and interested, either as a participant or as an informed spectator. Many of our students are eager followers of the sport pages, and can communicate with others in this area. Good conversant skills will aid the social phase of his future job placement success.

Enable your child to become well acquainted with your community. Take him about in your travels, and point out particular places of interest. This includes industry, and places of business in which later he may be employed. If you live in a small community, play a game with him as you drive by the various streets and see if he can name them. Repetition is proposed here. Whenever possible, use public transportation; later he may have to rely on this form of travel to commute to and from his job. The more orientation you can provide in this respect, the better he will be able to cope with this work transportation problem later.

Once our young adult enters the work study program and is placed in a work situation, concentrate more closely with him on homework assignments. The fact that he is participating in this program has markedly cut down his daily academic hours in the classroom. Therefore, certain areas may need extra reinforcement at home.

Specifically, you can assist the teacher-coordinator with his guidelines of budgeting the student worker's income. By all means, have your son or daughter set up a savings account; but equally important, see that he or she is active in the spending of the remainder of the income. Too often, parents are satisfied to see their young adults put the entire amount in the bank until the next payday. If we do this, we are not capitalizing on using these earnings as realistic learning devices for our students in the wise expenditures for their everyday needs and desires. If your child wants to buy a transistor radio, this if fine; but, let him plan for this item in his budget, and have him set aside a fixed amount each payday until the purchase day arrives.

Conversely, you might be willing to explore the advantages and disadvantages of credit buying with your more mature young adult. As a trial approach, let him make arrangements to charge an item at the local department store and casually supervise the monthly payments. Much learning will take place with this experience.

Equally valuable is the need that our young worker be properly outfitted for the job. Check the job description with the teacher-coordinator and make sure our young employee has the proper garment and shoes for the job. Be particularly alert when there is an outdoor work situation, and give attention to dress for extremely hot and cold weather. Moreover, make the care of work clothes a weekend project for the student. This might include washing uniforms, ironing, and polishing shoes.

In addition, keep close tabs on the health status of our young adult, for job attendance is important to job success. Make sure he is eating the proper foods at home and on the job and vigorously strive to keep him in good physical condition. He must realize that he can't afford to take days off for illness that could have been prevented. In this connection, work energetically with our adolescent to create a happy balance between work, rest, and recreation.

Finally, keep in close contact with the teacher-coordinator for your young worker's progress and problems. You can make a valuable contribution when work problems are channeled home that may never reach the classroom. Daily make it a point to discuss the work day with the student; if a problem is brought to the surface, get in touch with the teacher-coordinator immediately so he can take action. Likewise, if the teacher-coordinator shall call a parent meeting, it is vital that you be in attendance. Without question, he has something he wants to share with both of you, and he needs your earnest cooperation and assistance.

*Reprinted by permission from *The Pointer* For Special Class Teachers and Parents of the Handicapped. "Parents Can Help the Work Study Program," by Kenneth H. Freeland, Vol. II (No. 3), 1967.

During and after school hours, put your public relations to work in the community. Participate as often as you can in local civic, church, and service group projects. Open lines of communication and keep them open with local community agencies, both private and public. Work in close harmony and maintain effective relations with your Federal, State Labor, State Employment, and State Division of Vocational Rehabilitation contacts. Be constantly aware of what is happening, keep up-to-date, and get involved.

In taking this public relations aspect one step beyond, consider a few of the devices you might wish to incorporate into your program:

1. Work with your art teacher and class in an assembly-line production of an attractive Christmas card from the work study program. Using your mailing list, have your students address the envelopes and send them out to all the people concerned with your program.
2. Arrange an employer-student-employee dinner. Invite a guest speaker, and have one of your employers distribute your "Work Study Awards."
3. Set up a card system with all the birthdates of the people concerned with your program; include their addresses and names. Give the responsibility to a few of your students to send out the birthday cards with best wishes from the work study program.
4. At the end of the school year, have the class develop a thank you letter to all the people concerned with the program for their cooperation extended during the year. Duplicate the finished product and have the students address letters and envelopes from the mailing list.

Suggestions for the Substitute Teacher

The time will come when your program will be operating in high gear. You will have worked hard because it takes hard work. From this effort, you will have developed a certain spirit of cooperation from your students and from the many people associated with the program. When you reach this point, a pattern of routines will develop: routines that you have strived to reach, with every phase operating on a schedule that comes from planned organization. You will have problems, but you will eventually reach the point where you can deal with them with the objectivity of a true professional. The time will also come when you are ready to incorporate a new device or an innovation with your program. Each day will become more exciting and challenging than the previous day. However, periodically, there will be days when the program must function without your presence. You may be attending a conference, a workshop, or even home suffering with an illness. Regardless of the reason, you will want to be assured that your program is operating efficiently and your students have been well planned for. How is this accomplished? Quite easily if you have taken these following preparatory steps:

1. Your daily class schedule is posted in front of the room.
2. Your plan book is up-to-date.
3. Your teacher-coordinator weekly time schedule is current.
4. Your class work assignment list and time-transportation list are posted.
5. Your class student secretary has been briefed to assist the substitute on routine procedures.
6. *You have prepared a memorandum to the substitute* with some background on your program and suggestions that may assist him.

   What might this memorandum include to insure the program's smooth operation during your absence[12]?

   a. Start by welcoming the substitute to the class.
   b. Mention the location of your plan book, various schedules, forms discussed, attendance register, and class book.
   c. Mention your class secretary's name. She will assist regarding location of supplies and equipment.
   d. List the various keys and their locations (teacher's desk, tool locker, storage area, file cabinet, science table) .
   e. List by subject areas the texts and supplementary materials presently being used.
   f. Indicate the procedure for securing audiovisual aid equipment from the office.
   g. Indicate specific reference to the section of your plan book which has review lesson plans and certain areas that require periodic reinforcement with students. Include a brief description of the program.

h. Include a list of the other duties you may have (e.g., supervise study hall, room 124, third period on Tuesday while class is having art).

i. Include a current seating chart of the class.

j. Include assembly seating section assigned and location of class lockers.

k. List the name of the teacher next door in case the substitute needs assistance.

l. Terminate your memorandum by requesting the following be accomplished by the substitute: (1) Leave a brief note indicating the instructional areas covered. (2) List any particular problems confronted. (3) Note any telephone messages received concerning the program. (4) Insure that the attendance register is signed in the section designated.

m. Be sure to indicate that the substitute supply all information that you have requested. Have him replace this information in the envelope marked *For the Substitute Teacher*. Request that this envelope be placed in your mailbox with your room key since it is very possible that a different substitute teacher may be assigned the following day.

Your program should operate most efficiently in your absence if you have taken the preparatory steps listed above. However, it is imperative that all information for the substitute be kept up-to-date. The sealed envelope marked *For the Substitute Teacher* should always be kept in your mailbox. Insure that the person in charge of assigning substitutes for your school is briefed on the location and contents of this envelope.

Discussion Problems and Activities

1. In conducting your program, list other important areas not discussed.

2. Visit your school district's public relations man. He may have some ideas concerning your program.

3. What are the students' roles in the public relations program?

4. How would you diplomatically approach this problem?

One of your parents is exploiting the wages of one of your students.

5. What problems arise when the teacher-coordinator starts his rotation of workers within the school system?
6. Why should the teacher-coordinator pre-arrange the conference time with the parent?
7. What particular time of the day should you not attempt to confer with a cafeteria manager about one of your students?
8. List other public relations devices you might want to include in your program.
9. What particular area would probably give the substitute teacher the most difficulty in your program?
10. Would you advise the substitute to do any supervisory or coordinating work during his tour? If not, what would you suggest that he do during this time allotted?
11. Discuss and list the possible areas of the curriculum where the substitute might review and reinforce concepts previously explored with the class.
12. On the basis of their past performances, make a list of substitutes and their phone numbers that you would like to recommend to take your class upon your absence.
13. What particular advantages can you see if each of the district's special education teachers were to exchange assignments periodically during the school year for a day or two?
14. Do you think it would be wise to brief your students beforehand regarding their responsibilities in the event that they might have to work with a substitute teacher?
15. Discuss and plan an emergency *call system* with your students in the event that your high school is closed but the remainder of the school district is in session. Remember, your workers must get to their work experience and training sites on time as usual.

Chapter VII

REPORTS AND FORMS FOR YOUR PROGRAM

Most teacher-coordinators in the field will agree that an efficient reporting system is sound practice. It will enable you to maintain an accurate record of important data with reference to your program.[37]

Explanation of Reports and Forms

In this section, you will find a variety of field-tested forms and reports that may be helpful to you in your operation. Each will be discussed briefly as to how it can be utilized in your program. As you examine the Appendix, you will find that these forms have been completed in part to provide you with a better understanding of their usage. Some of the forms will include suggested reporting procedures in the lower left-hand corner.

FORM No. WSP-001. Title: *Index of Forms for School Work Study Program* (Table IX). This form maintains a record of the forms and reports used in your program. Assign each form a number to insure an effective record and filing system. *Indicate at the top center of each form used the name of your program, school, and address.*

FORM No. WSP-002. Title: *Work Study Assignment List* (Table X). This form is used to keep your principal, supervisor, and the payroll clerk up-to-date on your students' current work assignments. It indicates specifically various work experience, work training sites, and other necessary information.

FORM No. WSP-003. Title: *Work Study Time and Transportation Schedule* (Table XI). This form, when completed, is sent to the principal, supervisor, and the man in charge of transportation. This form indicates location and transportation for student during the school day.

Form No. WSP-004. Title: *Work Study Progress Report* (Table XII). A form similar to this one was used by a program in the Lansing Public School System, Lansing, Michigan.[15] This form includes a rating scale. It pinpoints specific areas where individuals may need additional assistance and guidance.

Form No. WSP-005. Title: *Work Study Progress Cumulative Report* (Table XIII). This form can be compiled every eight weeks from the information indicated on form WSP-004. At a glance, it will give you, your principal, and supervisor the various progress ratings on your students at any given time.

Form No. WSP-006. Title: *Student Work Study Record Form* (Table XIV). This is an individual record on each student indicating his various placement while in the program. Upon termination from the program, it is filed in the student's individual cumulative record folder.

Form No. WSP-007. Title: *Teacher-coordinator Daily Program Schedule* (Table XV). This form resembles the Daily Class Schedule. Copies should be on file with the principal and supervisor if changes should occur in the instructor's program.

Form No. WSP-008 Title: *Students' Employment Certificate Physical Check Form* (Table XVI). This form can be completed prior to the issuance of employment certificates each year. Most of the included information on your students will change each school year.

Form No. WSP-009. Title: *Students' Employment Certificate Check Sheet* (Table XVII). This form, initiated at the beginning of the school year, will insure that the instructor has the necessary information on record for all students applying for employment certificates.

Form No. WSP-010. Title: *Student Birth Certification Copy Form* (Table XVIII). This form, when completed, will insure that the teacher-coordinator has witnessed the student's birth certificate needed for the employment certificate. New students in the program should bring to class their birth certificates during the first few days of school so this form can be completed and filed.

FORM No. WSP-011. Title: *Student Payroll Information Form* (Table XIX). This form, when completed, will provide the payroll office with the needed information for students participating in the in-school work experience phase of your program.

FORM No. WSP-012. Title: *Student Payroll List Form* (Table XX). This form can be submitted to the payroll clerk indicating the hours of work and gross pay earned for a two-week period for the students participating in the work experience phase of the program.

FORM No. WSP-013. Title: *Student Individual Pay and Time Record* (Table XXI). This form was devised for students' individual use to give them experience in keeping a daily record of their hours worked and expected pay for a two-week period.

FORM No. WSP-014. Title: *Teacher-coordinator Payroll Accounting Form** (Table XXII). This is a helpful form to assist the instructor in accounting for the money expended for the work experience phase of the program. It also provides a reminder of the date the next payroll list is due.

FORM No. WSP-015. Title: *Students Ready for Work Training Form* (Table XXIII). This is a periodic report to the principal and supervisor. It indicates to the instructor and the above personnel the various students considered for work training placement in the community and what particular areas to be considered.

FORM No. WSP-016. Title: *Request for Handicapped Worker Application (State)* (Table XXIV). This is a sample form letter to secure the above application forms from the state labor office which issues these certificates.

FORM No. WSP-017. Title: *Rider Form to Accompany Handicapped Worker Application* (Table XXV). This form was devised to be attached with completed application forms so the certificate, if approved, would be forwarded to the school instead of the employer. This way the teacher-coordinator can deliver the certificate in person since many employers are unfamiliar with these certificates.

FORM No. WSP-018. Title: *Student Work Time Record* (Table

---

*Created by Richard Ferrand, former colleague and business manager. Form revised by author.

XXVI). This form is for the student to keep an individual account of the hours he works for a one-month period.

FORM No. WSP-19. Title: *Request for Handicapped Worker Applications (Federal)* (Table XXVII). This is a sample form letter which can be used to request applications through the Wage, Hour, and Public Contracts Division, U.S. Department of Labor in your locale.

FORM No. WSP-020. Title: *Student Information Form* (Table XXVIII). This form provides current information on student for job placement or can be included with letter of referral for vocational rehabilitation services. See *A Job Readiness Evaluation Check List,*[13] as compiled by Dr. John W. Kidd and colleagues.

FORM No. WSP-021. Title: *Job Training Lead Form* (Table XXIX). This is a useful form to list quickly various job leads for your program. It is advisable to leave a supply of these forms in the main office of the various schools for the teachers and other school employees in the event that they come in contact with various training sites for your program.

FORM No. WSP-023. Title: *School Work Study Summary Form* (Table XXX). This is a monthly report to your principal and supervisor indicating the various placements of students in your program.

REFERENCES

1. BEEKMAN, MARVIN: General principles of work-study programs. In Miller, Donald Y., and Danielson, Richard H. (Eds.) : *Work-Study for Slow Learners in Ohio.* Columbus, 1965, p. 18.

2. BREWER, JENNIE: Historical perspectives. In Younie, William J. (Ed.) : *Guidelines for Establishing Work-Study Programs for Educable Mentally Retarded Youth, 48* (10) :10, 1966.

3. CAMPBELL, ROALD F., *et al: Introduction to Educational Administration,* 2nd ed. Boston, Allyn and Bacon, 1963, pp. 294–319.

4. CHARNEY, LEON, and LaCROSSE, EDWARD: *The Teacher of the Mentally Retarded.* New York, Day, 1965.

5. DiMICHAEL, SALVATORE G.: Providing full vocational opportunities for retarded adolescents and adults. *Rehab, 30*:11–12, July-August 1964.

6. ESKRIDGE, CHARLES S., and PARTRIDGE, DONALD D.: Vocational rehabilitation for exceptional children through special education. *Exceptional Child, 29*:452–458, May 1963.

7. FREELAND, KENNETH H.: A new manpower source. *U S Golf Assoc Green Section Record, 4*:5, 6–8, January 1967.

8. FREELAND, KENNETH H.: Parents can help the work-study program. *The Pointer for Special Class Teachers and Parents of the Handicapped, 11* (3) :54–56, 1967.

9. FREELAND, KENNETH H.: A Suggestion for your labor problem. *Golf Superintendent, 35*:4, 24, 26, 28, 63, April 1967.

10. FREELAND, KENNETH, and REGER, ROGER: Brief report on disabled youth leaving school programs. *Cereb Palsy J, 29* (3) :9–12, May-June 1968.

11. KARNES, MERLE B.: Work-study programs for the mentally handicapped. In DiMichael, Salvatore G. (Ed.) : *New Vocational Pathways for the Mentally Retarded,* 1966, p. 31.

12. KELNER, BERNARD G.: *How to Teach in the Elementary School.* New York, McGraw, 1958, pp. 56–57.

13. KIDD, JOHN W.: A job readiness evaluation check list. *Exceptional Child, 33* (8) :581–583, April 1967.

14. KOLSTOE, OLIVER P., and FREY, Roger M.: *A High School Work-Study Program for Mentally Subnormal Students.* Carbondale, Southern Ill., 1965.
15. LANSING PUBLIC SCHOOLS: Parent's Handbook for Work Training Program for Mentally Handicapped (unpublished brochure). Lansing, Michigan, Everett High School.
16. LORD, FRANCIS E. (Ed.) : *Work Education for Educable Retarded Youth,* Report on Institutes. Los Angeles, Calif. State College, 1964.
17. MACKIE, ROMAINE P.: Teachers of Children Who are Mentally Retarded. Washington, D.C., U.S. Government Printing Office, Bulletin No. 3, 1957, p. 6.
18. NATIONAL EDUCATION ASSOCIATION, EDUCATIONAL POLICIES COMMISSION: *Education for All American Youth: A Further Look.* Washington, D.C., NEA, 1952.
19. NATIONAL EDUCATION ASSOCIATION, EDUCATION POLICIES COMMISSION: *The Purposes of Education in American Democracy.* Washington, D.C., NEA, 1938, p. 47.
20. PECK, JOHN R.: The work-study program—A critical phase of preparation. *Education and Training of the Mentally Retarded, 1*:68–74, April 1966.
21. PETERSON, RICHARD D., and JONES, EDNA M.: *Guides to Jobs for the Mentally Retarded.* Pittsburgh, Amer. Inst. Res. 1964.
22. REGER, ROGER: *School Psychology.* Springfield, Thomas, 1965, pp. 158–161.
23. ROTHSTEIN, JEROME H. (Ed.) : *Mental Retardation: Reading and Resources.* New York, Holt, 1964.
24. RUSALEM, HERBERT: The special teacher on the interdisciplinary team. *Exceptional Child, 26* (4) :180–181, December 1959.
25. SHAWN, BERNARD: Review of a work-experience program. *Ment Retard,* 2:360–364, 1964.
26. SLAUGHTER, STELLA S.: *The Educable Mentally Retarded Child and His Teacher.* Philadelphia, Davis, 1964, pp. 174–176.
27. STEVENS, GODFREY D.: An analysis of the objectives for the education of children with retarded mental development. *Amer J Ment Defic, 63*:225–235, September 1958.
28. SWITZER, MARY E.: The coordination of vocational rehabilitation and special education services for the mentally retarded. *Education and Training of the Mentally Retarded, 1* (4) :159–160, December 1966.
29. SYDEN, MARTIN: Guidelines for a cooperatively coordinated work-study study program for educable mentally retarded youth. *Ment Retard, 1*:91–94, 120, 124, April 1963.
30. U.S. DEPARTMENT OF HEALTH, EDUCATION, AND WELFARE: *Preparation of Mentally Retarded Youth for Gainful Employment.* Washington, D.C., U.S. Government Printing Office, 1959.
31. U.S. DEPARTMENT OF LABOR: *A Guide to Child-Labor Provisions of the Fair Labor Standards Act as Amended in 1966.* Washington, D.C., U.S. Government Printing Office, 1967, pp. 27–28.

32. U.S. DEPARTMENT OF LABOR: *Handy Reference Guide to the Fair Labor Standards Act as Amended in 1966.* Washington, D.C., U.S. Government Printing Office, 1966, p. 1.

33. U.S. DEPARTMENT OF LABOR: *Occupations in the Care and Rehabilitation of the Mentally Retarded.* Washington, D.C., U.S. Employment Services, Bureau of Employment Security, 1967, p. 61.

34. U.S. DEPARTMENT OF LABOR: *Schools Under the Fair Labor Standards Act as Amended in 1966.* Washington, D.C., U.S. Government Printing Office, November 1966.

35. U.S. DEPARTMENT OF LABOR: *State Child Labor Standards.* Washington, D.C., U.S. Government Printing Office, September 1965.

36. U.S. DEPARTMENT OF LABOR: *Training and Reference Manual for Job Analysis.* Washington, D.C., U.S. Government Printing Office, May 1965.

37. UNIVERSITY OF THE STATE OF NEW YORK: *Vocational Industrial Cooperative Programs.* State Education Department, Division of Industrial Education, Bureau of Trade and Technical Education, 1960, pp. 2–5,17,18,27,32,71.

38. VOELKER, PAUL H.: Curriculum implementation for the work-study program. In MILLER, DONALD Y., and DANIELSON, RICHARD H. (Eds.) : *Work-Study for Slow Learners in Ohio.* Columbus, 1965, p. 39.

39. WOLFENSBERGER, WOLF: Vocational preparation and occupation. In Baumeister, Alfred A. (Ed.) : *Mental Retardation.* Chicago, Aldine, 1967, pp. 232–273.

40. YOUNIE, WILLIAM J. (Ed.) : *Guidelines for Establishing School-Work Study Programs for Educable Mentally Retarded Youth, 48* (10) :10,31,61, June 1966.

APPENDIX

The names used on the forms and reports in this section are fictional. Any resemblance to persons living or dead, or to school work study programs in operation, is purely coincidental.

Form No. WSP 001

82   *Work Study Program for the Retarded*

Form No. WSP-002

TABLE X

WORK STUDY ASSIGNMENT LIST

Date:

From: Teacher-coordinator

To: Principal   Supervisor   **Payroll Clerk**   **File**

Subj.:   Work Study Assignment List

1. The following are the current assignments for the students of this group. Memorandum dated   *Oct. 5*   is hereby cancelled.

Student's Name	Assignment Work Experience	Hrs. Per Day	Pay Per Hr.	Current Age	Date Assigned
Abel, Thomas	*Cafeteria, North Elem.*	*3*	*$1.15*	*16*	*9/10/68*
Baker, Peter	*Washer, Bus Garage*	*3*	*1.15*	*16*	*9/10/68*
Charles, Ivan	*Maint. J.H.S.*	*3*	*1.15*	*16*	*9/12/68*
Fox, Elaine	*Cafeteria, S.H.S.*	*3*	*1.15*	*17*	*9/10/68*
George, Alice	*Office, Parks Elem.*	*3*	*1.15*	*17*	*9/11/68*
Hopp, William	*Laundry, J.H.S.*	*3*	*1.15*	*18*	*9/12/68*

Work Training

Jax, Gloria	*Hope Hospital*	*4*	*$1.50*	*19*	*9/16/68*
Kreb, Alex	*Drum Printing Co.*	*4*	*1.60*	*20*	*10/ 3/68*
Lass, Paul	*W. C. Holtz Co.*	*8*	*1.75*	*21*	*5/ 6/67*

Unemployed List
None

(One copy to each of the above and after every change to this list.)

Arnold Smith

Teacher-coordinator

Form No. WSP-003

TABLE XI

WORK STUDY TIME AND TRANSPORTATION SCHEDULE

Date:

From: Teacher-coordinator

To: Principal   Supervisor   Transportation Supervisor   File

Subj.:   Work Study Time and Transportation Schedule

1. Below is listed the time and transportation schedule for the students of this group. Memorandum dated   Oct. 5   is hereby cancelled.

WORK EXPERIENCE: IN-SCHOOL

Student's Name	Departs from Class	Destination (Job)	Returns to Class	Departs for Home
Abel, Thomas	*11:02* A.M.	*North Elem.*	*2* P.M.	*2:30* P.M.
Baker, Peter	*11:02*	*Bus Garage*	*2*	*2:30*
Charles, Ivan	*11:02*	*Junior High*	*2*	*2:30*
Fox, Elaine	*11:02*	*Senior High*	*2*	*2:30*
George, Alice	*11:02*	*Parks Elem.*	*2*	*2:30*
Hopp, William	*11:02*	*Junior High*	*2*	*2:30*

WORK TRAINING: OUT-OF-SCHOOL

Jax, Gloria	*11:02*	*Hope Hospital*	*No return*	*4* P.M.
Kreb, Alex	*11:02*	*Drum Printing Co.*	*No return*	*4*
Lass, Paul	*7:30 (home)*	*W. C. Holtz Co.*	—	*4:30*

(One copy to each of the above and after every change.)

Arnold Smith

Teacher-coordinator

Form No. WSP-004

TABLE XII

WORK STUDY PROGRESS REPORT

Date:

Student: *Thomas Abel*   Job Supervisor: *Mrs. G. Cook*
Firm Name: *North Elem. Cafeteria*

	RATING	
Does student follow directions?	2	Kindly use number scale below:
Does student accept constructive criticism?	3	
Does student sustain routine?	3	3 = Always
Does student get along with supervisor?	3	2 = Usually
Does student get along with coworkers?	3	1 = Sometimes
Does student see things to be done?	2	0 = Never
Does student appear to like his work?	3	Maximum Total = 63
Does student dress appropriately for the job?	3	
Does student come to work every day?	3	
Does student get to work on time?	3	
Is student a steady worker?	3	
Can student work by himself?	3	
Does student meet production schedules?	3	
Does student take care of tools and equipment?	3	Thank you for your excellent cooperation.
Does student do his share of work?	3	
Does student observe rules of the company?	3	*Arnold Smith* Teacher-coordinator
Does student observe safety rules and regulations?	3	
Is student courteous?	3	*554-3891* Phone
Is quality of student's work satisfactory?	3	
Does student practice good grooming habits?	2	
Are you satisfied with worker's progress?	3	
Total	60	

COMMENTS:

Geraldine Cook
_____
Job Supervisor's
Signature

(File in individual cumulative record folder at end of year.)

Form No. WSP-005

TABLE XIII

WORK STUDY PROGRESS CUMULATIVE
REPORT

Date:

Student's Name	1st (8 wks)	2nd (16 wks)	3rd (24 wks)	4th (32 wks)	5th (40 wks)	Total
Abel, Thomas	60	59				
Baker, Peter	57	58				
Charles, Ivan	48	50				
Fox, Elaine	56	57				
George, Alice	59	60				
Hopp, William	62	62				
Jax, Gloria	58	59				
Kreb, Alex	60	60				
Lass, Paul	62	61				

(Compiled from Form No. WSP-004 after each reporting period. Copies to principal and supervisor.)

Teacher-coordinator

Form No. WSP-006

TABLE XIV

STUDENT WORK STUDY RECORD FORM

Student's Name: *Baker, Peter*

Name of Employer	Job Title	Job Manager	Dates of Employment	Pay Per Hr.	Hrs. Per Day	Progress
Board of Ed. (James School Dist.)	Dishwasher Cafeteria	Mrs. Cook	9/67- 6/68	$1.00	2	Good
Board of Ed. (James School Dist.)	Washer Bus Garage	Mr. Dunn	9/68-11/68	1.15	3	Poor- Transf'd

COMMENTS:

11/12/68—Peter had difficulty in getting along with fellow workers.
(File in Student's Cumulative Record Folder.)

Form No. WSP-007

TABLE XV

TEACHER-COORDINATOR DAILY PROGRAM SCHEDULE

Date:

Period	Monday	Tuesday	Wednesday	Thursday	Friday	Notes
1	*Arith.*	*Free Period*	*Reading*	*Health*	*Free Period*	
Time	*8:09- 8:49*	*8:09- 8:49*	*8:09- 8:49*	*8:09- 8:49*	*8:09- 8:49*	
2	*Spelling*	*Science*	*Soc. Studies*	*Free Period*	*Reading*	
Time	*8:53- 9:33*	*8:53- 9:33*	*8:53- 9:33*	*8:53- 9:33*	*8:53- 9:33*	
3	*Soc. Studies*	*Reading*	*Free Period*	*Comp. Science*	*Spelling Arith.*	
Time	*9:37-10:17*	*9:37-10:17*	*9:37-10:17*	*9:37-10:17*	*9:37-10:17*	
4	*Music*	*Comp.*	*Comp. Pen.*	*Spelling Soc. Studies*	*Citizenship*	
Time	*10:21-11:01*	*10:21-11:01*	*10:21-11:01*	*10:21-11:01*	*10:21-11:01*	
5	*Lunch Period*	*Lunch Period*	*Lunch Period*	*Lunch Period*	*Lunch Period*	
Time	*11:01-11:46*					
6	*Work Study Supervision*	*Work Study Supervision*	*Work Study Supervision*	*Work Study Supervision*	*Work Study Supervision*	
Time	*11:46-*					
7	*and Co-ordinating Time*	*and Coordinating Time*	*and Coordinating Time*	*and Coordinating Time*	*and Coordinating Time*	
Time	*- 1:43*					
8	*Citizenship*	*Health*	*Arith.*	*Citizenship Pen.*	*Work Study Seminar*	
Time	*1:47- 2:27*	*1:47- 2:27*	*1:47- 2:27*	*1:47- 2:27*	*1:47- 2:27*	

Teacher-coordinator

(Send copy to principal and supervisor. One copy in Plan Book. Any changes, file new copies with the above.)

Form No. WSP-008

TABLE XVI

STUDENTS' EMPLOYMENT CERTIFICATE
PHYSICAL CHECK FORM

Date:

Student's Name	Age	Birthdate	Eye Color	Hair Color	Height	Weight	Health Status	Physical Defects
Abel, Thomas	16	8/5/52	green	black	5'6"	126	good	none
Baker, Peter	16	10/11/52	blue	brown	5'7"	130	good	none
Charles, Ivan	16	11/12/52	hazel	blond	5'8"	148	good	vision
Fox, Elaine	17	4/3/51	brown	blond	5'5"	115	good	hearing loss R.E.

Teacher-coordinator

(T-C file.)

Form No. WSP-009

TABLE XVII

STUDENTS' EMPLOYMENT CERTIFICATE

CHECK SHEET

Date:

Student's Name	Student Signature	Parent Consent	Employer Signature	Age Cert.	Medical Exam	School Entry	Employment Signed	Cert. Filed
Abel, Tom	yes	yes	yes	yes	yes	yes	yes	yes
Baker, P.	yes	yes	yes		yes			
Charles, I.	yes	yes	yes		yes			

Teacher-coordinator

(T-C file.)

Form No. WSP-010

TABLE XVIII

STUDENT BIRTH CERTIFICATION COPY FORM

Date:

Student's Name: *William Hopp*

(FILL IN BLANKS BELOW FROM STUDENT'S ORIGINAL CERTIFICATE.)

Texas   State Department of Health

Office of Vital Statistics at *Austin*

Department of Birth Registration

This is to certify that a birth certificate has been filed for

William J. Hopp
Name

Born on *10/3/50*   At *Austin*

Son of *Herman T.* and
(Father's Name)

Stella James
(Maiden Name of Mother)

Date Filed *10/12/50*   *J. R. Small*
(Local Registrar)

Number *56321460*

Teacher-coordinator

(File in Student's Cumulative
Record Folder.)

Form No. WSP-011

TABLE XIX
STUDENT PAYROLL INFORMATION FORM

Date:

Student's Name	Address	Social Security No.	Dependents Claimed	W-4 (IRS) Filed
Abel, Thomas	*10 East Ave.*	*143-02-6566*	*0*	*yes*
Baker, Peter	*202 Main St.*	*144-03-6567*	*0*	*yes*
Charles, Ivan	*63 Camden Dr.*	*145-04-4748*	*0*	*yes*

Teacher-coordinator

(One copy to Payroll Office; one copy T-C file.)

Form No. WSP-012
Budget Code: *650-12*

Pay Date: *March 3*
Period: From *Feb. 6*
To *Feb. 19*

TABLE XX

STUDENT PAYROLL LIST FORM

Students' Names	Date—				Feb.								Feb.						Total Hrs.	Rate	Gross
Day —	6	7	8	9	10	11	12	13	14	15	16	17	18	19						
	M	T	W	Th	F	S	S	M	T	W	Th	F	S	S			
Abel, Thomas	3	3	3	3	3			3	3	3	3	3			30	$1.00	$ 30.00
Baker, Peter	3	3	3					3	3	3	3	3			24	1.00	24.00
Charles, Ivan	3	3	3	3	3			3	3	3	3	3			30	1.00	30.00
Fox, Elaine	3	3	3	3	3			3	3	3	3				27	1.00	27.00
George, Alice	3	3	3	3	3			3	3	3	3	3			30	1.00	30.00
Hopp, William	3	3	3	3	3			3	3	3	3	3			30	1.00	30.00
																	$171.00

Feb. 20

Date Submitted   Teacher-coordinator   Payroll Clerk

Form No. WSP-013

Feb. 6					Arithmetic
Date		TABLE XXI			Subject
		STUDENT INDIVIDUAL PAY-TIME RECORD			
113		FORM			Ivan Charles
Room No.					Name

Day	Date Worked	Time		Hrs. Worked	Rate	Amount
		In	Out			
Mon.	2/ 6	11:30	1:30	2	$1.00	$2.00
Tues.	2/ 7	11:30	1:30	2	1.00	2.00
Wed.	2/ 8	11:30	1:30	2	1.00	2.00
Thurs.	2/ 9	11:30	1:30	2	1.00	2.00
Fri.	2/10	11:30	1:30	2	1.00	2.00
Sat.	2/11			No work		
Sun.	2/12			No work		
Mon.	2/13	11:30	1:30	2	1.00	2.00
Tues.	2/14	11:30	1:30	2	1.00	2.00
Wed.	2/15	11:30	1:30	2	1.00	2.00
Thurs.	2/16	11:30	1:30	2	1.00	2.00
Fri.	2/17	11:30	12:30	1	1.00	1.00
Sat.	2/18			No work		
Sun.	2/19			No work		

From: Date 2/ 6

To: Date 2/19

19 hrs.	Totals	$19.00

Checked: _____

Teacher-coordinator

(File in student's notebooks.)

Form No. WSP-014

TABLE XXII

TEACHER-COORDINATOR PAYROLL ACCOUNTING FORM

School Year

From:

To:

PAYROLL DUE DATE	1/26	2/9	2/23	3/9	3/23	4/6
ACTUAL PAY DATE	2/3	2/17	3/3	3/17	3/31	4/14
DATES OF PAY PERIOD	1/9-1/20	1/23-2/3	2/6-2/17			
1. Possible work days this period	10	10	8			
2. Total work hours available	4315	3850	3397			
3. Total work hours this period	465	453	295			
4. Hours left (item 2 minus item 3)	3850	3397	3102			
5. Cost for period (rate per hr. times item 3)	$465	$453	$295			
6. Cumulative cost (item 5 + previous item 6)	$4036	$4489	$4784			

(This figure will increase each pay period until you reach your total budgeted figure for the school year.)

(T-C file.)

Form No. WSP-015

TABLE XXIII

STUDENTS READY FOR WORK TRAINING FORM

Date:

From: Teacher-coordinator

To: Principal   Supervisor   File

Subj.: Students ready for work training placement within the community.

1. The following students are available for *full-time* placement:

Names	Age	Area of Interest
None		

2. The following students are available for *one-half* day placement:

Names	Age	Area of Interest
Mary Jones	*19*	*Nurse's aide*
James Jackson	*19*	*Mail room worker*

(One copy each to principal, supervisor, and file every 10 weeks.)

Teacher-coordinator

Form No. WSP-016

TABLE XXIV

REQUEST FOR HANDICAPPED WORKER

APPLICATION (STATE)   Date:

From:_____,   _____
      (Employer's Name)   (Employer's Address)

To: Division of Labor Standards
     Dept. of Labor
     State of_____

     _____
     Att'n.:

1. Kindly send the necessary application forms for a Certificate to Employ Handicapped Worker at a Wage Less than the Minimum in accordance with Article_____ of the Labor Law to the Teacher-coordinator at the Work Study Program listed below.

2. It is also requested that if the subject application is approved by your office that the subject certificate also be forwarded to the Teacher-coordinator below.

3. Thank you.

                    _____
                    (Name of Teacher-coordinator)

                    _____
                    (Room No.)

                    _____
                    (School)

                    _____
                    (School Address)

                    _____
                    (Employer's Signature)

(One copy T-C file.)

Form No. WSP-017

TABLE XXV

RIDER FORM TO ACCOMPANY HANDICAPPED WORKER APPLICATION (STATE)

School Work Study Program

From:_____   _____
    (Teacher-coordinator)   (School)

To: Division of Labor Standards   _____
    Dept. of Labor   (Room No.)

    State of_____   _____
                        (School Address)

_____   _____
Att'n.:   (Town)   (State)   (Zip)

                      _____
                        (Date)

Subj.:_____,   _____
    (Employer's Name)   (Employer's Address)
attached Application for a Certificate to Employ Handicapped Worker at a Wage Less than the Minimum Under Article_____of the Labor Law.

1. This is to certify that_____, _____
                           (Name of Student)   (Age)
    who resides at_____
                        (Address)
    named on the attached application is currently enrolled in our Work Study Program at the above school.

2. Prior authorization from the above employer in a letter to your office dated _____requests that, if the attached application is approved, the subject certificate be forwarded to the above school.

3. Thank you.

                      _____
                        Teacher-coordinator

Certificate issued on_____
                    (Date)

(One copy to T-C file.)

Form No. WSP-018

TABLE XXVI

STUDENT WORK TIME RECORD

For:_____ _____
(Month)   (Year)

	Sun	Mon.	Tues.	Wed.	Thurs.	Fri.	Sat.	Total Hrs. Worked
Date		1	2	3	4	5	6	
Hrs.		0	3	3	3	3	0	12
Date	7	8	9	10	11	12	13	
Hrs.	0	3	3	3	3	3	0	15
Date	14	15	16	17	18	19	20	
Hrs.	0	3	2	3	3	3	0	14
Date								
Hrs.								

TOTAL HRS. MONTH

Mary Jones

_____   _____
(Date)   (Student's Name)

(T-C file.)

Form No. WSP-019

REQUEST FOR HANDICAPPED WORKER

APPLICATIONS (FEDERAL)

_____
(Date)

From:_____
      (Teacher-coordinator)

To: Wage and Hour and Public Contracts Division
     United States Department of Labor

_____

_____
Att'n.:

Subj.: Handicapped Worker Certificate; Request applications concerning.

Ref.: (a) Fair Labor Standards Amendments of 1966 (P.L.89-601, 80 Stat.830)

      (b) Regulations contained in WHPC Publication 1183, dated Jan. 21, 1967.

1. In accordance with the regulations contained in References (a) and (b), please forward the necessary application forms to employ_____students below the
                                           (No.)
minimum wage.

2. Thank you.

_____
Teacher-coordinator

(T-C file.)

Form No. WSP-020

TABLE XXVIII
STUDENT INFORMATION FORM
Date:

Name_____Sex_____Tel. No._____
Address_____Age_____Birthdate_____
Who supports student?_____
Father's name_____Mother's name_____
Father's occupation_____Place of employment_____
Student's selective service classification_____ Local Board No._____
Student's disability_____ Can student use public transp.?_____

Names of Brothers and Sisters	Age	Living at Home	In School	Married	If Employed, Where?

Last school attended_____ Highest grade_____
School district_____ Teacher_____
Subjects liked best_____ Years in program_____
Activities_____ Attendance_____
If left school, reason?_____
Intelligence test: Date_____ Test_____ Score_____
Achievement Level: Reading_____ Arith._____ Spelling_____ Other_____
Is student now in good health?_____ (If not, explain on reverse side.)
Is student presently under medical or psychological treatment?_____ If so, by whom?_____
Height_____ Weight_____ Hair color_____ Eye color_____
Personal grooming habits: Good___ Fair___ Poor___
Speech: Adequate___ Articulation___ Stutter___ Voice quality___ Projection___
Hearing: Normal___ Mild loss___ Moderate loss___ Severe loss___
Vision: Good___ Fair___ Poor___ Wears glasses___
Motor Coordination: Large muscle: Good___   Fair___   Poor ___
                     Small muscle: Good___   Fair___   Poor ___
Ability to accept authority: Good___ Fair___ Poor___
Ability to accept criticism: Good___ Fair___ Poor ___
Behavior: Cunning___ Deceitful___ Underhanded___
          Boisterous___ Loud___ Ill-mannered___
          Quiet___ Well-mannered___ Cooperative___ Respectful___
          Dependable___ Trustworthy___
Sociability: Withdraws___ Distant___ Self-centered___
          Amiable___ Reserved___ Slow to make friends___
          Quiet___ Respectful___ Cooperative___
Work Habits: Careless___ Poor in application___ Steady___ Needs direction___
          Industrious___ Little direction needed___ Completes tasks___
Does student have birth certificate?_____ Social Security No._____
Area of occupational interest_____ Jobs performed at home_____

Did student participate in school work study program?_____
If yes, state briefly student's progress._____

Student's Work Study Record:

Employer	Phone	Kind of Work	Dates of Employment	Pay Per Hr.	Hrs. Per Day

_____   _____
Phone   Teacher-coordinator

Form No. WSP-021

TABLE XXIX

JOB TRAINING LEAD FORM

Date:

From: *Mrs. John Jones*

To: *Mr. Arnold Smith*
      Teacher-coordinator

Subj.: Job Training Lead; Information concerning

Please contact: *Mr. Paul White*

Title: *Personnel Manager*

Company: *T. W. Holt Co.*

Address: *152 East Ave.*

Phone: *262-3156*

Type of Work: *Stock Room Helper*

Comments:
Willing to train young fellow part-time.

(Distribute and file completed copies in T-C File.)

Form No. WSP-023

TABLE XXX

SCHOOL WORK STUDY SUMMARY FORM

Date:

From: Teacher-coordinator

To: Principal   Supervisor   File

Subj.: Work Study Summary Report for month of *March.*

	TOTALS
I. No. OF STUDENTS IN PROGRAM	17
II. WORK EXPERIENCE	
In-school (½ day, with pay)	9
In-school (½ day, no pay)	
Out-of-school (weekends)	
Other:	
III. WORK TRAINING	
Out-of-school (½ day, with pay)	2
Out-of-school (full-day)	2
Out-of-school (evenings)	
Other:	
IV. VOCATIONAL EVALUATION, TRAINING, AND PROJECTS	
Vocational Exploratory Program at Voc. Center	1
Vocational Program at	
Vocational Evaluation (DVR) at Rehab. Center	1
Personal Adjustment Training (DVR) at	
On-the-job Training (DVR) at Harris Dairy	1
State Apprentice Program at Braun Mason Co.	1
Training Project at	
V. UNEMPLOYED (List names)	0
None	
TOTAL*	17

*If total does not equal item I, explain below.

_____

Teacher-coordinator

INDEX